THE INSTRUCTIONS OF GAMPOPA

A Precious Garland of the Supreme Path

CW00552113

The Instructions of Gampopa

A Precious Garland of the Supreme Path

Ven. Khenpo Karthar Rinpoche

Translated by
Lama Yeshe Gyamtso

Edited by
Laura M. Roth and David N. McCarthy

ROOT TEXT BY GAMPOPA
Translated by
Lama Yeshe Gyamtso and Laura M. Roth

Snow Lion Publications
Ithaca, New York

Snow Lion Publications
P.O. Box 6483
Ithaca, New York 14851 USA
607-273-8519

Copyright © 1996 Karma Kagyu Institute

All rights reserved. No part of this book may be reproduced by any means without prior written permission from the publisher.

Printed in the United States of America

ISBN 1-55939-046-8

Library of Congress Cataloging-in-Publication Data

Khenpo Karthar Rinpoche, 1924-
The instructions of Gampopa: a precious garland of the supreme path / oral commentary by Khenpo Karthar Rinpoche; root text by Gampopa; translated by Yeshe Gyamtso; edited by Laura M. Roth and David N. McCarthy.
p. cm.
ISBN 1-55939-046-8
1. Sgam-po-pa, 1079-1153. Lam mchog rin phreṅ. 2. Spiritual life—Buddhism. 3. Spiritual life—Dwags-po (Sect) I. Sgam-po-pa, 1079-1153. Lam mchog rin phreṅ. II. Roth, Laura M., 1930- . III. McCarthy, David N. IV. Title.
BQ7775.K48 1996
294.3'444—dc20 95-52951
CIP

Contents

Preface

A Precious Garland of the Supreme Path is a collection of twenty-eight lists of points of advice for practitioners of the Buddhadharma at every stage of practice, by the twelfth-century teacher and founder of the Kagyu lineage of Tibetan Buddhism, Gampopa. The commentary by Ven. Khenpo Karthar Rinpoche was presented orally to a group of his students at Karma Triyana Dharmachakra (KTD), the Karma Kagyu Monastery in Woodstock, New York, in the closing days of 1991. The teaching was translated by Lama Yeshe Gyamtso.

Gampopa lived from 1079 to 1153 C.E.[1] He was born in central Tibet, and was trained as a doctor, but when his family succumbed to an epidemic, he promised his wife on her deathbed that he would become a monk and devote his life to Buddhism. Gampopa was ordained as Sonam Rinchen at the age of twenty-six, and he was trained in the Kadampa tradition that originated with Atisha.[2] This tradition taught a graded path to enlightenment, emphasizing a thorough grounding in the self-discipline and basic meditation of the hinayana, as well as training the mind in loving-kindness, compassion, and the view of emptiness at the mahayana level. Later he met the great yogi Milarepa and became his foremost student. Milarepa's teacher, Marpa the translator, had brought the vajrayana or tantric teachings of the *mahasiddhas* from India, including the six yogas of Naropa, in a system known as *mahamudra,* the "great seal."[3] Gampopa thus combined the Kadampa tradition with the mahasiddha tradition from India. He established a monastery at Gampo Dar (whence his name), where he gathered many students, who later founded a number of schools of the Kagyu lineage. In particular, the Karma Kagyu lineage arose from Gampopa's student Dusum Kyenpa, the first Karmapa, who founded Tsurphu Monastery, the present home of his seventeenth incarnation, His Holiness Urgyen Trinley. Other main works of Gampopa are *The Jewel Ornament of Liberation*[4] and *The Four Dharmas of Gampopa.*

Ven. Khenpo Karthar Rinpoche has been abbot of KTD in Woodstock since its inception in 1978, and is spiritual director of a number of affiliate centers. He was born in Kham in eastern Tibet in 1924, was ordained as a monk at the age of twelve, and was trained at Thrangu Monastery. He taught at Rumtek Monastery in Sikkim, India after leaving Tibet in 1959 with His Holiness the Sixteenth Karmapa, and in 1975 was recognized as a *Chöje Lama* or Superior Dharma Master. Rinpoche's first book, *Dharma Paths,* was published by Snow Lion Publications in 1992.

Lama Yeshe Gyamtso was born in Canada, and is a student of Kyabje Kalu Rinpoche. He completed two three-year retreats under the direction of Ven. Lama Norla. He has translated extensively for Kalu Rinpoche, Khenpo Karthar Rinpoche, and other lamas, and has given Buddhist teachings himself. He is known for his clarity and precision in communicating the Buddhist teachings.

David McCarthy is a long-time student of Khenpo Karthar Rinpoche who has worked for several years on a project to transcribe and edit Khenpo Karthar's teachings. We wish to thank Michael Erlewine for his support of David during his work on this text. I am Professor Emeritus of Physics at the University of Albany, and have also been a student of Khenpo Karthar Rinpoche for some years. I previously edited Rinpoche's book,

Dharma Paths, published by Snow Lion in 1992. We gratefully acknowledge the help of Pat Dinkelaker and John Fudjack of Troy, New York, who transcribed most of the tapes, and helped with editing. We also wish to thank Robert Walker for making a number of helpful editing suggestions, and Willard D. Roth, director of Karma Kagyu Institute, for sponsoring my work on the project.

The Tibetan text of *A Precious Garland* was taken from the block print edition produced at Rumtek Monastery. Lama Phunsok Bist, the chant master of Rumtek Monastery, entered the Tibetan text into the computer, for which we thank him. Our translation of the root text was made during the summer of 1995 at KTD. An early translation of the same work was included in Evans-Wentz's *Tibetan Yoga and Secret Doctrines*, and we recently became aware of an independent translation by Eric Pema Kunsang.[5]

As usual in Buddhist works, there are a number of Sanskrit and Tibetan words as well as references to Buddhist concepts. We have tried to explain unusual terms when they appear, but since there are now many books available on the Dharma, we have not felt it necessary to include a glossary. Many readers will know the basic terms and ideas, and for those who do not, a number of books have glossaries of Buddhist terms, including Khenpo Karthar's *Dharma Paths*.

We hope that the words of Gampopa and the commentary of Khenpo Karthar Rinpoche will benefit many students of the Buddhadharma.

Laura M. Roth

The Instructions of Gampopa: A Precious Garland of the Supreme Path

COMMENTARY BY VEN. KHENPO KARTHAR RINPOCHE

The author of *A Precious Garland of the Supreme Path* was Lord Gampopa, who was also known as Dagpo Rinpoche or Lord Sonam Rinchen. Lord Gampopa is considered the father of the Kagyu tradition—the root and basis for its existence. His activity in this regard began in a previous life in which he was a bodhisattva named Chandra Prabha Kumara or "Youthful Moonlight," who was a student of Buddha Shakyamuni. Lord Buddha predicted in the *Samadhiraja Sutra* that during the age of decadence[6] Youthful Moonlight's incarnation would propagate the teachings of that sutra, which are the true meaning, the mahamudra. Through his aspiration as a bodhisattva and the blessings of Lord Buddha Shakyamuni, Youthful Moonlight was reborn in Tibet as Lord Gampopa, and created what we know as the Kagyu lineage.

In his life as Lord Gampopa, he composed a variety of *shastras* or commentaries on the Buddha's teachings. Two of the most notable are *The Jewel Ornament of Liberation* and *A Precious Garland of the Supreme Path*. Of these two especially, but also of his other works, Gampopa said that for those in the future who have strong faith in him, studying these texts would be exactly the same as receiving teachings directly from him. He said that although future students would not have the opportunity to meet him personally, he could not convey more to them than what is in these texts.

The text of *A Precious Garland of the Supreme Path* begins with the Sanskrit words *namo ratna guru*, which mean, "I pay homage to the precious *lama*." This homage is to Gampopa's root gurus, principally Lord Jetsun Milarepa, as well as to his other gurus who embody the qualities that he is going to set out. In the Tibetan text that follows, he pays homage to the holders of the stainless practice lineage, whose splendor radiates like the light of the sun throughout space, as a result of their having developed three qualities. The first is that, externally, they engage in the proper conduct that liberates them and enables them to bring others to liberation. Second, they have internally realized the vast, ocean-like, innermost, profound meaning of the Dharma. Third, their aspirations to benefit beings have come to maturity, enabling them actually to help others.

At this point Gampopa requests that the holders of this stainless practice lineage, who possess such inconceivable qualities, engulf both him and his followers in their splendor. This refers to his immediate students and those in the future who will practice this tradition.

Next, Gampopa explains that the glorious speech of the Kagyupas consists of the precise instructions in the correct view, meditation, and conduct. He himself heard these instructions, properly considered them, and, not only that, he put them into practice. Being tormented by overwhelming compassion for all beings, he set out these instructions for the benefit of his students and future followers. In writing this text Gampopa displayed the skill of his consummate compassion, fulfilling the actions of a holder of the lineage of the buddhas, and directly benefiting sentient beings.

1 The Ten Causes of Loss

Gampopa says that those in the future who wish to obtain liberation and the state of omniscience, or complete buddhahood, should constantly remember the ten causes of loss.

The first of the ten causes of loss is wrongdoing. The point here is that the only possible cause for experiencing human existence, which is the basis for the practice of Dharma, is keeping pure moral conduct. Since very, very few beings preserve any form of genuine morality, very few beings attain a human existence. Generally speaking, people do not practice that which is virtuous, but engage in that which is harmful—in wrongdoing. Until wrongdoing is relinquished, a person will never attain liberation from suffering or even liberation from the lower realms of existence, let alone omniscience, and will have no ability to benefit others in any way. Therefore, the first thing that is a cause of loss is wrongdoing.

The second cause of loss is wasting this precious human existence, which has what are known as the eight freedoms and the ten resources.[7] It is important to appreciate that only in this precious human existence, with these eighteen characteristics, does a being actually have the ability to practice Dharma. The first cause of loss involves actions that will prevent birth as a human being in general. Here, we are concerned especially with those actions that will prevent us from experiencing that particular type of human existence called "the precious human existence," that is, human existence that possesses the eight freedoms and the ten resources.

The third cause of loss is meaningless distraction and meaningless busy activity. The age in which we live is called an age of decadence. Among the aspects of its decadence is the fact that our vitality is very weak. There are very few factors keeping us alive and very many factors that will, at some point, lead to our deaths. Furthermore, death can be experienced very suddenly and through any number of causes. Thus, it is important to remember that there is no time to waste. Therefore, the third cause of loss is activity that merely wastes time and is a distraction.

The fourth cause of loss is addictive conceptuality and the ensuing afflictions. It is said that the very nature of the mind as it is—the mind in itself—is the *dharmakaya*. All the qualities of the dharmakaya are spontaneously present within us. They are what we really are. However, not recognizing this, we tend to follow after addictive thoughts and concepts that occur in the mind. We get ensnared by the mental afflictions that they generate, and this prevents our recognition of the mind.

The fifth cause of loss is the situation in which we easily grow tired of relying on a teacher and practicing his or her instructions. It is important to understand that the only possible basis for our attainment of liberation from the intense suffering of *samsara* is receiving and practicing the special instructions of our lamas. To disregard the value of receiving and practicing such instructions in order to engage in various sorts of meaningless activity is the fifth cause of loss.

The sixth cause of loss is the situation in which a practitioner impairs or destroys any or all of the three vows. In general, it can be said that the only vessel in which we can cross the ocean of samsaric suffering and reach the realm of great bliss, the realm of liberation, the state of buddhahood, is the excellent vessel of the three types of vow or commitment. These are: 1) the external vow of individual liberation (*pratimoksha* vow); 2) the internal vow of *bodhicitta* (*bodhisattva* vow)[8]; and 3) the vajrayana vows or *samaya*. Allowing these vows to become impaired through intense mental afflictions (*klesha*) or mere carelessness is a cause of loss.

The seventh cause of loss is to discontinue following the instructions and practice after having gained a slight amount of realization through relying on a spiritual friend or guru. Having had some realization, you may become easily distracted by meaningless activity, abandon the instructions and practice, and thereby inhibit the further growth of experience and realization.

The eighth cause of loss is the situation in which, having no genuine realization yourself, but having heard a great deal of the profound speech of the *siddhas* of the lineage, you repeat their speech to many people in order to attract students and become wealthy, popular, and powerful. You deceive many people by pretending to have realization. This is the eighth cause of loss.

The ninth cause of loss is activity that harms other sentient beings. This should be avoided because all sentient beings have been our parents and, as our parents, they have been extremely kind to us. Another reason is that altruistic bodhicitta is the spinal cord of the path to liberation. Losing it is to lose the entirety of the path. Therefore, it is necessary to let go of all spitefulness toward others, and especially all that is actually harmful to others. It is important to remember that the generation and flourishing of bodhicitta depend entirely upon interaction with other sentient beings. Therefore, it is necessary to have all sentient beings as objects of compassion and actually to generate compassion for those beings.

The tenth cause of loss is procrastination, and what is lost is body, speech and mind—the three gates. Specifically, when you are young and your body is strong, your mind clear, and your speech supple, you do not engage in the practice of Dharma because you feel impelled to engage in mundane activities. While doing so, you think, "I will practice Dharma when I get older, when things have settled down a bit." Then, not having practiced when you were young, you find when you get older that you cannot practice because you do not have the habit of doing so. You are not as strong as you were, it is harder to learn things, and so forth. This type of procrastination is definitely a cause of loss.

These are the ten things that are causes of loss.

2 The Ten Necessary Things

Gampopa then presents ten things that are necessary in order to practice Dharma. The first of these is a stable commitment to the practice of Dharma in general, and to continuing the specific format of practice you are doing until you finish it. If you do not have this commitment, you will be easily swayed by the opinions, advice, and conversation of others, and you will not get anything done. In order to maintain a strong commitment, you must have a detailed and accurate knowledge of the essential points of the practice you are doing. This commitment will arise through considering the previous ten causes of loss.

The second thing that is necessary is, through faith and diligence, to accomplish the wishes and instructions of your lama. Faith is a delight in practicing and accomplishing the instructions you are given because you recognize the benefits of doing so. Diligence is a delight in going through the actual process of accomplishing these instructions in which you have faith. Through the possession of this strong faith and intense diligence you are able actually to put the instructions of your lama into practice.

The third thing that is necessary is to put the instructions of your lama into practice faultlessly, with skill and understanding. Although the instructions are without defect, the way you implement them could be defective. For example, if you attempt to practice secret *mantra* without having any renunciation for samsara and without having generated any bodhicitta, then although the instructions of secret mantra are profound and faultless, your practice of them will have the defect of being totally ineffective and will not generate any qualities whatsoever. Therefore, it is important to put Dharma into practice in a skillful way, with an understanding of the correct sequence of practice.

The fourth thing that is necessary is to persevere in practice through a correct insight into the meaning of the teachings and a strong confidence in the teachings. This means putting the instructions of the lama into practice without mistaking their meaning and in accordance with the lama's intentions of how they should be practiced. This is where *sherab* (or *prajña* in Sanskrit)—which means knowledge—comes in because it is only by means of an inquisitive insight into the meaning of the instructions you receive that you will be able to practice them properly.

Furthermore, this practice must be prolonged until you generate the full extent of qualities that are possessed by your lama and come to the same realization as your lama. You persevere in practice by means of a stable faith or confidence in the value and efficacy of the practice. Thus the fourth thing that is necessary is correct perseverance in practice through insight and confidence.

The fifth thing that is necessary is to maintain mindfulness, attentiveness, and carefulness. You must be mindful of what conduct to adopt and what to abandon. You must be attentive and aware of the extent to which you are employing mindfulness. Finally, you must be careful to repair any lapses or deviations you may make from mindfulness and attentiveness.

If you apply these three qualities, your body, speech, and mind will be unstained by the defects of faulty conduct. If, on the other hand, you lack mindfulness, you will not remember what is to be adopted and what is to be abandoned. If you lack attentiveness, nothing in your conduct will allow you to pay attention to what you are doing. Even if you remember what you should be doing, you will not be able to do it because you are lost. If there is no carefulness, when you start to get lost in faulty conduct, you will have no way to bring yourself back because you will not have the habit of paying careful attention to what you are doing. The result of lacking these three qualities is that your vows and samaya will be impaired. Therefore, before you meet with the enemies of distraction, you must gird yourself with the armor of mindfulness, attentiveness, and carefulness, so that when you are "attacked" you will not be destroyed.

The sixth thing that is necessary is also made up of three points: the armor of commitment, courage, and stability in practice. Through the armor of commitment, you do not waiver in your commitment to practice. Through courage, the obstacles and problems that arise during life or during practice do not affect you. You do not allow these obstacles and problems to dissuade you or turn you away from practice. Through your commitment and courage, you build a stability in your practice that is unwavering and devoid of fear, and that prevents you from being pulled away from practice by suddenly arising conditions. If you allow yourself to be turned aside from practice by the slightest little incident, obstruction, or interruption, then you are worse off than any worldly person. People in mundane activities have great forbearance when faced with interruptions and obstacles. Thus it is all the more important for people practicing Dharma to show that same commitment and courage.

The seventh thing that is necessary is freedom from attachment (*chag may*) and the absence of addiction (*zhen may*). The Tibetan phrase for this quality means, literally, "not letting your nose-rope be grabbed by others." A nose-rope is used on a cow so it can be led easily. If you are free of any kind of attachment or addiction to specific places and people, to your possessions, to pleasant experiences of the five senses, or to desirable objects that can be experienced with the five senses, then you are in control of yourself and no one else can control you. However, having attachment to pleasant conditions and particular situations is the same as having a ring through your nose with a rope attached to it and handing the end of the rope to someone else who can pull you wherever they want you to go. Only by wrapping your nose-rope around your own head and not giving it to someone else can you practice Dharma.

The eighth thing that is necessary is that your practice be embraced by threefold excellence. The first of the three excellences is pure motivation in the beginning. At the beginning of any session of practice you generate the thought or intention that through this practice all sentient beings may be brought to the state of complete buddhahood. The second excellence is that during the main body of the session you maintain an even placement of the mind in a state free of elaboration, free of conceptual reification of the practice. The third excellence is that at the end of the session you seal the practice by the dedication of not only the merit accumulated in that session but also the merit accumulated by all sentient beings in the three times—past, present, and future. All merit is dedicated to the complete liberation and omniscience of all beings.

If your practice is embraced by this threefold excellence in the beginning, the middle, and the end, it results in the twofold accumulation of merit and wisdom. By means of the correct motivation, meditation, and dedication, you gather the accumulation of merit. By means of sealing the entire practice through nonconceptuality that is free of elaboration, you gather the accumulation of wisdom.

The ninth thing that is necessary is the firm development of loving-kindness and compassion, through which you benefit others in both direct and indirect ways. Loving-kindness is the desire that all sentient beings possess happiness and the causes of happiness. Through loving-kindness, you engage in the conduct that is necessary in the short run to bring direct benefit to beings. For the long run, and as the indirect benefit, you make the aspiration that, through your practice, all sentient beings may come to attain the supreme happiness of the state of buddhahood. Compassion is the desire that all sentient beings be free from suffering and the causes of suffering. With this motivation you benefit sentient beings directly by freeing them from situations of suffering, and indirectly through the aspiration that your practice be a cause of their total liberation from all the sufferings of samsara.

The tenth necessary thing is that through the application of knowledge or insight (*sherab*) you avoid the defect of reification. This consists of, first, the intellectual understanding, and second, the realization or direct experience, that all the things we experience possess no substantiality and no inherent characteristics. The first is understanding that all things we experience are, from their own side, unestablished as anything other than mere experiences—they are mere elaborations or fabrications. The second is the correct full realization that the actual nature or way of abiding of all things is without elaboration, that is, free from being stained by their apparent characteristics.

This text is divided into lists of ten, and we have now covered the first two of these. A proper understanding of each set depends on the recollection of the previous set. The meaning of the second set is best found by an examination that is grounded in an understanding of the first set, and what we go through as we continue will be based on understanding what we have gone through previously. For example, if you were to look at one of the later lists of ten, it would not make much sense out of the context of the material that precedes it. Therefore please do not forget these first two sets of ten.

3 The Ten Things Upon Which to Rely

Next I will discuss the ten things on which we must rely in order to generate the qualities associated with Dharma practice, so that the virtues we cultivate in the practice of Dharma will flourish and we will not be hindered or afflicted by any defects.

The first thing on which we must rely is a holy *guru* who possesses both realization and compassion. The lama must possess realization because a teacher who has no realization or actual experience is like a painting of water, which cannot quench our thirst, or a painting of fire, which cannot warm us. As well, the lama must possess compassion. If the lama merely has realization but has no compassion, he or she cannot teach and will not help sentient beings develop virtuous qualities and relinquish defects. Thus the first thing on which we must rely is a lama who possesses both realization and compassion.

The second thing on which we must rely is a solitary, pleasant, and splendorous place of practice. Having completely received instructions from the lama described above, we must rely on such an environment in order to put those instructions into actual practice. The environment should have four characteristics: First, it must be a place of solitude. We must be somewhat isolated from distractions; otherwise we will not be able to practice at all. Second, it must be pleasant, and this means a place where we are not afflicted by excessive cold or heat or other things that disturb both the mind and body and become obstacles to practice. Third, it should be splendorous, which means a place that has been engulfed by the splendor of the siddhas of the lineage. If possible, it is best to practice in an environment where the great practitioners of the past have practiced. If not, it is sufficient to practice in a solitary and pleasant place. Fourth, the environment should be a wilderness or wild place. The Tibetan term is *gompa,* which also means monastery. But here it does not mean a formal monastery where there are *stupas* and where lamas, monks, and nuns are living. It means a place that is a reasonable distance from other habitations and not in the middle of a city where we would be greatly distracted.

The third thing on which we must rely is companions who are in harmony with ourselves in view, in conduct, and in strength of attitude. The first characteristic, harmony of view, means that the people with whom we live and practice should be committed to attaining liberation, just as we are. The second, harmony in conduct, means that our companions and friends also abide by whatever level of external discipline is appropriate, whether that of a fully ordained monk or nun, a novice, or a lay disciple. The third characteristic, having a strong attitude, means that they are free of the paranoia that can create situations of intense disharmony that conflict with the aims of practice. In other words, we should not be living with people who are constantly thinking, "He is angry at me. She is jealous of me. I didn't like the way they said that. They're causing problems. I had better get rid of them," and so forth. They should not be of a mind-set that creates disharmony. Thus the third thing on which we must rely is companions who possess these three characteristics. If we rely upon such companions, rather than being sources of distraction our companions will help us to attain liberation, and we can help them as well.

The fourth thing is that we must rely on moderation in sustenance, having recognized the defects of excessiveness. If we are not moderate in what we require in the way of food, clothing, and so forth, we will go crazy from seeking after these things. Moderation consists of having enough clothing and shelter that we do not freeze or burn, and enough food that we do not starve to death. The point is to use these external conditions to sustain ourselves in order to practice. We should avoid worrying a great deal about whether or not things are pleasant—for example, the taste of the food we eat. It is recommended that we conceive of our sustenance as if it were medicine. When you are taking medicine to cure an ailment you do not think, "I like this medicine. It tastes good, it is sweet. I do not like that medicine; it does not taste very good." You take it because it will remove whatever illness you are suffering from. In the same way, you should eat and drink to survive, so that you are able to practice, and not to enjoy the taste of the food. In addition, if you are constantly trying to acquire better food, better clothing, and so forth, the effort of trying to acquire these things creates a great deal of hardship. Then, if you acquire them, they become sources of distraction because your mind is directed toward enjoying them rather than practicing the Dharma. You end up being tormented by attachment. Thus it is important to be careful and mindful in your use of external resources.

It was said by the Buddha that if you eat more than you need, it becomes an obstacle to meditation. You begin to feel heavy, and so much of your energy is directed towards the process of digestion that there is none left for meditation. It is recommended that you fill one third of your stomach with food, fill one third with liquid, and leave one third empty. The point is not to measure the amount of food going in, but simply to be appropriate in your consumption and to keep it regular.

The fifth thing is that we must rely impartially on the instructions of the lineage of siddhas. This means not to be too choosy, not to think, "I have to rely upon this, but I will leave that out. I can forget about that. It doesn't apply to me. I don't need that." It means to have an impartial respect and veneration for all the authentic instructions that come from the various lineages of awakened *yogis*. It is important to receive formally the transmission (*lung*) and the instruction (*tri*) for whatever we are studying. However, it is appropriate as well to read texts of profound instruction that we come across. It is good to do so impartially because at this point we do not know what is going to spark realization in us. We do not know yet what kind of instruction we might come across that might click and generate an understanding of the nature of the mind. Therefore, it is important not to reject any authentic instruction that comes our way.

The sixth thing is that we must rely on substances, medicines, mantras, and various conditions that are beneficial to ourselves and others. Do not develop the attitude, "I am a yogi of great realization; therefore, I don't need anything. If I get sick I don't need medicine. I don't need to be careful in any kind of external way." Since you have not perfected your realization, you are somewhat at the mercy of your body, which is composed of the four elements. Therefore, you have to generate the conditions that support the equilibrium and balance of the elements, which brings about good health. You should not reject correct medical treatment and so forth—the various profound conditions that are beneficial to your state of health. In the same way you should not reject these things for others. You should not think that there is something shallow or unimportant about benefiting others through giving them medicine, food, and other common things, because all of these are of genuine benefit to others if they are appropriately administered. You should not think, "I am a yogi following the yogic tradition. I can reject science. I can reject medicine. These are worldly things of no lasting meaning." Actually, these are things that can be of great benefit and should not be rejected out of hand.

The seventh thing is that we must rely on food that is in accordance with our state of health and constitution, and methods of approach to practice that are in accordance with our capabilities. Concerning food, it is not important whether or not you especially like the food you eat. If a food is sweet and delicious yet harmful to your health, you should avoid it. If you find a food distasteful but very beneficial to your health and longevity, you should rely upon it.

Concerning the practice of the Dharma, it should be in accordance with your understanding and ability. If someone has a very limited attitude and is terrified of the profound acts and the profound understanding of the bodhisattvas, it is suitable for that person to practice the lesser vehicle, because he or she will naturally be attracted to the peace of liberation and wish to escape the sufferings of samsara. It would be inappropriate for such a person to go directly into the practice of mahayana. In the same way, someone who has reached the point of being able to practice the mahayana, yet who has no faith in or real understanding of the vajrayana or secret mantra, should practice the mahayana, and in particular the sutrayana. The vajrayana teachings are especially profound and can lead to the state of unity, the state of Vajradhara[9] in one lifetime, yet this cannot happen to someone who has no faith in them and has no insight into their true meaning. For this reason, although ultimate buddhahood is attained eventually through the practice of secret mantra, the Buddha did not simply teach that one vehicle. He taught all the various stages and methods so that sentient beings of various faculties can be gradually matured to the point where they can practice these ultimate teachings.

The eighth thing is that we must rely on meditation techniques and modes of conduct that actually help our experience of practice. We should practice in such a way that we are focusing our attention on the practice we are actually performing, and not mixing up that practice with other things that are inappropriate in that context. For example, if you are practicing tranquility meditation or *shamata*, it is important that you continue with the practice until you generate certainty about its benefit and a certain stability of mind, at which point you can go on and practice insight or *vipashyana* meditation. However, if in the midst of shamata practice you start performing the analysis associated with vipashyana practice, then you destroy your fledgling practice of shamata. You do not get anywhere, because you are not practicing what you set out to practice. In the same way, if you are doing a simple practice that does not rely upon extensive analysis, then while it might seem appropriate to engage in a complicated analysis, it would not be. If you are engaged in a practice that depends on some analysis, then discarding that analysis and simply resting in a state of simplicity would harm your practice, although it would be appropriate in another circumstance.

With regard to the mode of conduct, it is important that what you do, your physical position and so forth, be appropriate to the practice you are doing. The most obvious example is that if you are doing the first part of *ngöndro*, the preliminary practices,[10] you do not sit as you would during shamata practice, but you do prostrations and so forth. Furthermore, you recite the refuge prayer while you are doing prostrations—you do not practice shamata. It is important that every aspect of your practice be harmonious and unified.

The ninth thing on which to rely is worthy students who have faith and respect, and this is to be relied upon by someone who, having attained some of the qualities associated with the path, is functioning as a teacher or spiritual friend for others. When you genuinely start to have these qualities, you have to decide in what situations it is appropriate to teach and how much is appropriate to teach. The decision should not be based on how many people you can possibly get together to teach, and how much you could possibly manage to say to them. You should choose what you say to whom based upon what is actually appropriate and necessary for them.

Generally speaking, students of the Dharma should have the three kinds of faith. The first is the faith of clarity, which is a clear sense of the value of Dharma and therefore a natural, sincere delight in it. The second, the faith of desire, is the intense desire to attain the qualities that are possessed by the buddhas and bodhisattvas. The third type of faith is confidence or trust, which is the conviction on the student's part that Dharma is a better way to live and that practice is a worthy way to spend one's time. With regard to respect, students should be able to recognize their own defects and appreciate the qualities of their teacher. Respect in the context of Dharma instruction means that students should regard their teacher in the same way they would regard a doctor, who prescribes the appropriate medicine for someone who is suffering from a serious illness.

It is important that the teacher abandon two extremes. One is to think, "I am a yogi who has transcended mundane activity. Therefore, no matter how many qualified students approach me I am not going to tell them anything, because I am beyond such communication with other people." If qualified students appear and you are qualified to teach, you should do so. The other extreme is to think, "I am a yogi with some qualities. Therefore, I should teach whatever I can to everyone I meet." The danger of the second extreme is that when you teach people who have no respect for the Dharma, what you teach is wasted because the people are not benefited by it. Not only are they not benefited by the teaching, but because they receive it without faith and respect, their lack of respect for Dharma and for their teacher actually grows as time goes on. Thus teaching carelessly is a very effective way of sending both yourself and others to the lower realms.

The tenth thing on which we must rely is continual mindfulness and attention throughout the four types of activities. The four types of activities are: eating, going to sleep, walking, and sitting. We should be mindful of what we are doing in all situations, highlighted by these four, and attentive to maintaining this mindfulness. It is particularly important to protect all of our vows, whatever they are, and our samaya. We should regard the protection of vows and samaya the way we would regard the protection of a tremendously important jewel we are keeping. If we knew that outside somewhere there were thieves waiting for a chance to steal this jewel, we would constantly be on our guard, watching for the thieves who are trying to sneak in and steal the jewel. In the same way, to maintain our discipline we must constantly watch our minds, because the thieves who will steal the jewel of our discipline are the mental afflictions that arise in the mind. When mental afflictions take over the mind, they start producing afflicted thoughts and concepts, which lead to acts of wrongdoing. Thus it is especially important to watch the mind at all times.

There are both common and uncommon explanations for how to maintain mindfulness and attention throughout the four activities. The common explanation is that when you are eating, eat moderately as was explained before. When you go to sleep, go to sleep with the virtuous intention of getting up the next morning and using all your time for the practice of the Dharma. When you are walking, be careful of stepping on insects or harming other sentient beings. When you seat yourself, be careful that you are not sitting on any insects hidden under the cushions, or harming any beings. That is the way the common mindfulness is directed.

The uncommon mindfulness of secret mantra is based upon these and includes these, but adds to them other practices: When you are eating, consider your body as the *mandala* of all the victorious ones, and offer your food to them as feast substances. When you are going to sleep, meditate on the clear light associated with sleep, which may make use of reciting a mantra, resting the mind in a state of nonconceptuality or nonfabrication, and so forth. When you are walking, visualize your root guru above your right shoulder so that you conceive that you are circumambulating him. When you are seated, visualize your root guru above your head at all times. The point of both the common and uncommon explanations is to preserve mindfulness and attention at all times, because these are the ground or basis of all Dharma.

These are the ten things that are to be relied upon from the beginning of your practice of Dharma until your attainment of the complete fruition. The first of these, of course, is the correct teacher. The ten things should be relied upon so that you are never without them, the way your body is never separated from its shadow.

4 The Ten Things to Be Abandoned

The next list is the ten things that must be abandoned. The first of these is a teacher or a master all of whose actions are mixed with the eight worldly dharmas.[11] Although such teachers may give very profound explanations and be very learned, all they are concerned with and all they direct their actions toward is acquiring possessions for themselves and their retinue, acquiring praise, being served, and becoming famous. They are tremendously concerned with avoiding the loss of any of their personal possessions, avoiding any kind of criticism, and avoiding situations where people will not serve them. They are very much afraid of getting a bad reputation. Although they may look good and speak well, and be learned in the information aspect of Dharma, they have no realization and are not genuine teachers. They should therefore be abandoned.

The second thing that must be abandoned is "retinue" and companions who harm your state of mind and harm your practice. Retinue refers to students, if you are a teacher, and if you are in a position of authority, to those under your authority in either a spiritual or mundane sense. Companions means friends, people you live with, family, and so forth. It is important to stay away from people who present obstacles to your practice and generate mental affliction in you that is of no use. There is a traditional saying in the Kagyu lineage, "Get away from your birthplace." This is because in the place of your birth there are usually people to whom you are tremendously attached and people for whom you have tremendous aggression. For this reason yogis have tended to wander about, going to uncertain places where people do not know them. Because no one knows them, there are fewer interruptions to their practice. You may think it is necessary to continue to associate with people you are attached to, but that is not the case. You cannot really help them because if they destroy your practice, they are harming themselves and you, and you end up harming them and yourself as well.

The third thing that must be abandoned is places that are either very distracting or dangerous. Even if you have abandoned your place of birth, if you go somewhere else where there are a lot of mundane things you can do rather than practice, where there are a lot of desirable experiences you can have other than practice, this will be an obstacle to practice. In fact, it is no better than being in your birthplace. On the other hand, even if you are in a place of solitude, it may be a place where there is the danger of not obtaining healthy food and water, or danger from large carnivorous animals or small poisonous animals. In a place where there is danger to life or health you will not be able to practice because you will be afraid and anxious. This fear will prevent you from relaxing, and without a relaxed mind, practice cannot progress.

The fourth thing that must be abandoned is sustenance that comes from theft, robbery, deception, or concealment. Theft refers to stealing something in a hidden manner. Robbery refers to stealing something through superior force. Deception refers to pretending to have qualities you do not have, that is, getting someone to give you something as an offering by pretending to be worthy of offering. Concealment refers to concealing defects you do have, again in order to obtain support. These four improper ways of obtaining food and other conditions necessary to live as a practitioner must be abandoned.

As well, you should abandon all sustenance that arises from improper activity on the part of others. Even if people give you something without any kind of wrongdoing on your part, if they stole it or got it through some sort of deception and you know that, then you should not accept it; you should not partake of it.

What should be relied upon is food and support that is obtained without wrongdoing, in an honest and direct manner. When you are practicing Dharma it is appropriate to receive gifts, offerings, food, or whatever you need to live on from others, if others are willing to give them. It is even appropriate to beg for alms, but you should be honest and direct about what you are doing. If you have no food you can say, "I have no food. Would you give me some?" and if they wish to, they will; but there cannot be any kind of deception.

The fifth thing that is to be abandoned is work and activity that harms our state of mind and harms our practice. It is appropriate to engage in meritorious work and activity, such as erecting, repairing, or making offerings for monasteries, images of the Buddha, and so forth. Physical activity connected with merit is fine because it actually benefits the mind in the long run. But meaningless activity that distracts us and actually drags the mind downward should be avoided.

The sixth thing that should be abandoned is food, conduct, and activity that are harmful to our health. Our physical bodies possessing the eight freedoms and the ten resources are extremely precious. They are the basis for our human existence. We should prolong our lives as much as possible so that we can make use of this opportunity to practice the Dharma. It is therefore important to avoid food and activity that will either cause sickness or otherwise put us in danger of untimely death.

The seventh thing that must be abandoned is fixation and attachment to desirable things or situations that bind us with our own greed. This means being attached to the acquisition and protection of possessions, amusements, wealth, fame, and so forth. It includes both the feeling that we need these things and the anxiety we feel at the danger of their loss, because both are fixations on these things and the experiences associated with them. Our fixation on these conditions means that not only will their presence not help our good qualities increase, but it will also cause them to decrease as time goes on. For this reason it is important to avoid places and people to whom we are unduly attached or on whom we are unduly fixated.

The eighth thing that must be abandoned is careless conduct that is the cause of other people having no faith in the Dharma. This does not mean activities that are directly harmful to others, which have already been discussed in earlier lists. It refers to the situation in which practitioners have actual experience, or even some realization of the meaning of Dharma, and therefore have little anxiety as to what other people may think of them. They might be inclined to act a little strangely. But it is not appropriate for practitioners to indulge in displaying their realization in this manner, because other people, whether they are involved in Dharma practice or not, will see their actions as defects. They will not think, "These people act odd; they must have realization." They will think, "Even the most serious Dharma practitioners, people who are supposed to have realization, seem to have personal defects," and that will cause them not only to despise the practitioners but also to despise the Dharma. This leads other sentient beings to accumulate the extremely harmful negative karma of abandoning and reviling the Dharma. Therefore it is important, no matter how high your experience and realizations are, to be externally subdued, disciplined, and proper in your conduct.

The ninth thing to be abandoned is activities that are of no benefit to ourselves and others, like running around and sitting around. This means to abandon meaningless journeys —for example, visiting a big ocean or a high mountain just for sightseeing purposes—and to abandon meaningless entertainment. These things are a waste of time, and you do not necessarily have much time to waste. Thus, if you determine that a specific activity or action will not be of real benefit to yourself or to anyone else, you should avoid it.

The tenth and last thing to be abandoned is concealing our own defects and proclaiming or advertising the defects of others. It is important not to try to conceal our own defects through stealth, and not to focus on the defects of others, making them clear to everyone. We must always make the aspiration to be as beneficial as possible to others, and we should conduct ourselves in accordance with that aspiration. Our goal is to be able to remove our own faults, not conceal them, and to help others remove their faults, not advertise them. We especially do not wish to become arrogant. The basis for arrogance, and the way to maintain arrogance and cause it to flourish, is to conceal our own defects and expose those of others. The difference between a genuine Dharma practitioner and a worldly person is that the worldly way is to conceal our own defects and advertise those of others, while the Dharmic way is to conceal the defects of others and advertise our own.

These are the ten things that are to be abandoned.

5 The Ten Things Not to Be Abandoned

Next are the ten things not to be abandoned. To begin with, compassion should not be abandoned because it is the very root of any benefit we are able to give to others.

The second thing not to be abandoned is appearances. Since appearances are the natural display of the mind, it is unnecessary to abandon them. Tilopa indicated this when he said, "It is not by appearances that you are fettered, but by fixation on them. So abandon that fixation." It is not what you experience that causes confusion, it is your fixation on the experience as being inherently what it appears to be. Therefore only this fixation need be relinquished, not experience itself.

The third thing is that thought is not to be abandoned, because it is the play of the ultimate nature or *dharmata*. As is said in the Kagyu lineage prayer, "The nature of thought is the dharmakaya." If we are capable of looking directly at the essence of thought, then whatever thought arises is self-liberated. If we can put this into practice, there is no need to try and remove thoughts or abandon them in any way.

The fourth thing not to be abandoned applies primarily to those with realization. Mental afflictions are the indication of wisdom and therefore need not be abandoned. The presence in our experience of stupidity, aversion, pride, desire, and jealousy indicates the presence in our continuum of the wisdom of the *dharmadhatu*, the mirror-like wisdom, the wisdom of equanimity, the discriminating wisdom, and the wisdom of activity. Since the mental afflictions are merely the display of the wisdoms that are their essence, someone who has the realization to experience this directly need not abandon them.

It is important to analyze this statement because it might seem very strange on the face of it. Just a few minutes ago you were told that you must definitely abandon mental afflictions, and now you are being told you do not have to abandon them. This is not a contradiction, but a demonstration of the difference in the maturity of practitioners at various levels of the teachings. The approach for beginners, in which it is necessary to abandon mental afflictions, is like the need for stairs. Someone who does not have wings and who wishes to get to the second story must walk up a set of stairs. The process of walking up stairs is like the process of subduing the mental afflictions. Someone who has wings like a bird does not need to use stairs but can fly directly up to the second story. Having wings corresponds to having the realization to be able to implement the profound wisdom of secret mantra. Thus, these two pieces of advice are not contradictory but are directed toward individuals at different levels of practice.

The fifth point in this section is in the same category as the fourth. The desirable objects that appear to the five senses are not to be abandoned because they are the water and manure of experience and realization. For a practitioner with some realization and some strong experience, there is no coarse fixation on his or her imputed inherent existence. There is no coarse ego-clinging, and in the absence of that, there is no feeling or inherent concept of ownership. For such yogis and yoginis, no matter how many things surround them, no matter how much wealth or prosperity they experience, they do not have a feeling of identification with or ownership of these things. It is just as though there were beautiful wild animals wandering around them. If we see wild animals, we do not feel, "That's my tiger," or, "That's my deer." We can appreciate them, but there is no fixation on them.

For example, when Jetsun Milarepa was offered some very hearty nutritious food, it was of great benefit and enhanced his realization tremendously, but he did not develop any attachment to the taste of it. It was not a question of indulging his desire, it was a question of strengthening his body. In the same way, advanced practitioners can use food and drink as feast substances. There are, as well, practices in which the clothing they wear is consecrated as the armor of mantra. These are practices that are suitable for advanced practitioners with some direct experience. It is important to understand that different pieces of advice in this text are offered to practitioners at different levels.

The sixth thing that is not to be abandoned is sickness, suffering, and pain, because they are excellent teachers. When we become distracted and engage in wrongdoing, or when we are simply not mindful, or not experiencing stable renunciation, sometimes a little bit of suffering can remind us very directly and effectively of what is to be avoided, what is to be renounced, and what suffering really is. For example, if we experience a certain amount of physical difficulty as a human being, then we might consider how much more unpleasant it would be to be reborn in the lower realms, where the sufferings are much worse. That might inspire us to try to avoid rebirth in the lower realms. Therefore, such difficult situations need not be avoided, because at times they can be very helpful.

According to Shantideva, our experiences of suffering can be of benefit because they sadden us, and the sadness brings us back in on ourselves and cuts through our pride. Through the loss of our coarse arrogance we are able to experience genuine compassion for others. We think, "If I am suffering this much, if it's this unpleasant, how must it be for others?" and we come to appreciate the suffering of others. This leads us to avoid wrongdoing and that which is harmful to ourselves and to others, and leads to a natural delight in that which is virtuous. Thus there is some benefit to such experiences.

The seventh thing that is not to be abandoned is enemies and obstructers, because they naturally exhort us to practice. From the mahayana point of view, the basis of our attainment of buddhahood, our realization of the ultimate nature, is the cultivation of such qualities as patience. The only possible way we can cultivate the virtue of patience is through situations in which we are dealing with some misfortune or actual aggression. For that reason, people who are aggressive to us are our assistants in practice, and since they arise naturally they are said to be the natural exhortation to practice. They are also the exhortation that leads us to the realization of the true nature of all things, which is buddhahood.

However, if enemies and obstructers disappear spontaneously, it is a sign of attainment (*siddhi*) and you do not have to reject that result. If unpleasant situations disappear even though you make no special effort to remove them, you do not have to try to get them back again. If you have merit and attainment, in many instances this will cause situations in which others are aggressive to you to be pacified naturally. When that happens, you do not have to think something has gone wrong. For example, when the king attempted to kill Acharya Nagarjuna with a variety of swords by hacking away at his neck, the king was not able to hurt Nagarjuna because Nagarjuna did not have the karma to be hurt. In the same way, someone with realization will not naturally find many enemies and obstructions, and that is a sign of siddhi; it is a sign of attainment. Just because the presence of enemies may not always be bad, this does not mean that the lack of enemies is necessarily bad.

The eighth thing not to be abandoned is methodical, step-by-step progress in our study and practice, because this is what raises us to the height of definitive understanding. We should not think that a gradual progress through the various stages or vehicles of practice is to be abandoned because it may not seem to be the final meaning of the Buddha's teachings. Such thinking is incorrect. All of the great scholars and siddhas of the past became learned in all of the various stages and vehicles of the Buddha's teachings, and on the basis of that, finally arrived at the definitive understanding associated with the vajrayana. For our own development we must practice in a way that will gradually ripen or mature our insight into the meaning of Dharma. There are many stages to this and they should all be cultivated. As well, we should not abandon or revile the various presentations of Dharma that are made in different styles or at different levels, because these are all appropriate for the needs and dispositions of different beings.

The ninth thing not to be abandoned is the various Dharma practices involving physical activity, because these are genuine practices that mature the mind and are beneficial. This means not to abandon prostrations, circumambulation, and other external practices of Dharma because these actually do benefit us; they actually do bring results.

The tenth thing not to be abandoned is the intention to benefit others, even when you do not have much ability to benefit them directly right now. Often, when people begin to practice they think, "What is the benefit of saying, 'I am doing this practice in order to benefit others. I will benefit others in the future in such and such ways?' Since I am not actually doing anything that benefits others right now, what meaning is there? I cannot do anything that will help anyone." In fact, there is the same potential for this altruistic attitude to produce the actual results as there is for a seed to produce a flower. If you say there is no benefit in altruism, then it is like saying a seed will not produce a flower. Just as altruism in itself is not a benefit to others, a seed is not a flower. A seed is not even a sprout. Nevertheless, without a seed there is no possibility of having the sprout and leaves and flower, so it is important to begin with the attitude and intention that you will be of great, vast benefit to others.

At the beginning of the path no one can perform the vast acts of a bodhisattva. When the Buddha first generated the intention to attain supreme enlightenment he was unable to do much to help others. As time went on, though, he became extraordinarily capable of helping others. Nowadays, people have a great deal of doubt about this. When instruction is given in such matters as bodhicitta, people commonly say, "What possible use is this? I can't do anything." It is important not to abandon altruism merely because you do not seem to be able to do so much now.

These are the ten things not to be abandoned.

QUESTIONS AND ANSWERS

Q: I have a question about the common and uncommon forms of mindfulness. Do these apply to the beginning, when we start to eat, start to fall asleep, or start to walk, or through the whole process of walking or eating? Are they for beginning points or continuous?

A: Whether you practice the common or uncommon ways of developing mindfulness, it should be as continuous as possible. Of course, because you engage in a variety of activities, it is not possible to remain continuously absorbed in one particular contemplation or one particular meditation. However, you should do it at the beginning of any activity, and then do it whenever it comes to mind as the activity continues, whether it is eating, walking, or other activity. The more continuous it is, the better. It is not the case that you simply generate the visualization or contemplation at the beginning and then forget it.

Q: I am not sure I understand the three types of faith. I believe the first type was the faith of clarity and the second type was the faith of desire. Does that mean the desire to become enlightened, or is there more to it than that?

A: Yes, that is right. There might be some confusion about the term "desire." This type of faith, the faith of desire, is recognizing the value of obtaining liberation and omniscience or buddhahood. The thought, "I really want to attain that state, and therefore I will do whatever is necessary to attain it," is different from conventional or mundane desire, in which we want pleasant experiences of all kinds. The faith of desire is not based on a mistake or a misconception; it is based on wanting that which is actually worthwhile. Although the manner of thought is in a sense parallel to conventional desire, the object is completely different.

Q: Of the ten things to be abandoned, the eighth one was abandoning activities that cause loss of faith in the Dharma. Could you clarify whether that refers to our own loss of faith in Dharma or others' loss of faith in the Dharma through seeing our actions?

A: The point of the eighth of the ten things to be abandoned is to abandon bizarre conduct that causes other people to have disrespect for the Dharma. This can arise when you have some kind of experience in the practice that leads you to feel an urge to act in an odd way. In that case it will harm you because it will be misleading, and it will harm others. Or you might have some degree of realization that leads to acting in an odd way. This may not harm you but it might harm other people, because other people cannot see your realization; they can only see what you are doing. If you do things that appear odd or strange or improper to them, they will assume that there is something wrong with you, and, since you are supposed to be an exemplary practitioner, that there is something wrong with the instructions or the path that has led you to behave in such a way. You are causing sentient beings to have disrespect for the Dharma, which turns them away from Dharma and is a tremendous source of bad karma for them. The responsibility of someone with realization is to hold and foster the Buddhadharma, to cause it to flourish, and to be a teacher and example to others. If you act in such a way that you cannot do that, then you are not upholding your responsibilities.

Q: I wonder if you could give some examples.

A: I can give an example of myself. I am always talking about how important loving-kindness and compassion are, but I eat meat all day long.

Q: You have commented on many powerful points made by Gampopa in this text. Is it possible or necessary for us to put all these points into practice?

A: First of all, Gampopa gives a variety of instructions and raises a large number of points in this text because the entire text is not intended for one person. It contains methods and instructions designed to guide individuals from the beginning of their path until they reach the state of full buddhahood. It also contains instructions designed for different types of individuals. You have to make a distinction between studying the text and putting it into practice. In the context of study and analysis of the text, it should be done in its entirety—reading the text through from beginning to end and coming to a definitive understanding of it as a cohesive work. On the other hand, when you put it into practice, you select portions of it as personal advice that are appropriate to your own situation. In the context of practice, it is not important to go through the whole text from beginning to end and remember each and every thing in it.

Q: In the first list, the ten causes of loss, the term "meaningless" was used in terms of meaningless activity and meaningless distractions. Does this mean that many of the things we do should be avoided, such as watching TV, listening to music, or taking a nap? Is that what is termed "meaningless activity"?

A: From a conventional, mundane point of view, of course, when you are very tired from work and all the kinds of activities that you have no choice but to perform, you might need to relax. Normally, in the world, we do not consider it a waste of time to see a performance of some kind or just relax and take a nap. The issue here is that we do not have much time to practice, and we do not want to waste what little time we have. It would definitely be meaningless activity, a cause of loss or waste, if having committed yourself to spending a certain amount of time every day on Dharma practice, you did not do that, but instead used the time to relax and goof off.

Q: The question that I have relates to developing courage and confidence in the practice of Dharma in the face of obstacles. I am a householder with a child, and I am working. I tend to have the habitual pattern of not being able to practice every day at the same time. I know that consistent practice is important. Contemplating the four thoughts as is done at the beginning of ngöndro practice, I should be sensitized to the fact that this is a precious human life, that life is impermanent, that the law of karma is true, and that we should not attach ourselves to the pleasures of the mundane world. Yet, still being driven by habitual patterns, it is hard to have time to do formal practice. What is the best way to work with this and become a stronger practitioner?

A: To one extent or another everyone has to deal with this situation. The main thing in working with this is, as I said earlier, not letting anyone get hold of your nose rope, which means to be in control of your own direction and your own decisions. Someone who has complete conviction about these four thoughts that turn the mind will not have any trouble practicing Dharma. If you find that, although you understand them, you cannot seem to practice because things always get in the way, it indicates that either you do not completely trust them or you are afflicted by hopes and fears. Even though we have studied impermanence and we have studied the defects of samsara, we tend inside really to hope we will not die for a long time, and that gives a feeling of some room, some time to wait for practice. Although we have studied the defects of samsara, inside we really doubt whether it is so bad, and doubt makes it easy to defer practice. If someone has complete conviction about the validity of the four thoughts that turn the mind, he or she will not have any trouble practicing.

The fact that you have access to the Dharma and that you are involved in these practices indicates that you have accumulated a lot of merit in the past, which means that you have a store of merit on which to build the habit of Dharma practice, and that will counteract the habit of not practicing. Thinking of Dharma at all, thinking of such things as the four thoughts that turn the mind, thinking, "I have to find time to practice," indicates a previous habit of Dharma practice. That is something you can trust in yourself and it is something you can build on.

As far as actual practice, the main thing to be practiced is ngöndro, which we call preliminaries. Actually the term ngöndro is somewhat misleading because it implies that these are sort of minor preliminary things to be gotten out of the way so you can get on to the real stuff. Usually people have the idea that after they finish ngöndro there is going to be something else much better, much more effective, and certainly much more interesting. But this is incorrect, because the topics brought up and the techniques presented in the ngöndro are the essence of all Dharma—they are not really preliminaries at all. In particular, going for refuge and generating bodhicitta are the basis and essence of the entire practice of Dharma. Bodhicitta is the removal of obscurations. Bodhicitta is the attainment of enlightenment.

The further practices as well are extremely central. Vajrasattva practice is the removal of obscurations, the various habitual patterns and confusion that obstruct the practice of Dharma and are the whole reason for which we have to practice in the first place. The accumulation of merit through the mandala offering leads directly to the relinquishment of ego-clinging, the false imputation of an inherently existent self, and this is what Dharma is all about. Finally, the guru yoga is the ultimate and final way to perfect all qualities and remove all defects. The essence of Dharma is the realization that your mind, in its nature, has always been and will always be the dharmakaya itself, and it is guru yoga that sparks this type of experience and realization.

If you understand the efficacy, centrality, and profundity of ngöndro, you will have delight in it and respect for it, and therefore you will be able to practice it as much as possible. Now, if you have a lot of responsibilities—for example, you have to work, you have a home, a child to take care of, and so forth—your time is more limited than that of someone with no responsibilities. But no matter how many responsibilities you have, if you really want to practice, you will definitely find at least some time for it, and the desire to practice leads to the creation of opportunities to do so. Otherwise, if there is not a strong, intense desire to practice as soon as possible, you find yourself procrastinating. The cause of procrastination is simply a lack of motivation, and the way to overcome the habit of procrastination is to practice. The more you practice, the more you will want to practice, and you create a habit that snowballs, that reinforces itself. Thus, the best thing for you to do is keep on practicing, keep on going, and that itself is the solution to the problem of not being able to practice. There is no other solution needed. The more you practice, the more you will benefit not only yourself, but everyone who comes in contact with you, especially your children and those who live with you.

Q: You said that we do not have to abandon our enemy because he might teach us patience. Suppose a man has a wife who will not let him study Buddhism or associate with the lamas or teachers, and will not let him teach his children about Buddhism because she and everyone else around him are

Christians. Should this man abandon his enemy the way the Tibetans had to leave Tibet after the Chinese invasion, or should he practice Buddhism quietly and patiently in his home and not speak to his children about Buddhism until, perhaps in the future, the chance arises that he can do so?

A: I cannot definitely say what such a person should do. If that person can be patient with whatever he is subjected to by his wife, that is the best thing, because patience is the most effective way of increasing our own personal qualities. On the other hand, if he cannot be patient with the situation and it is certain to lead to aggression on his own part, and is certain to lead to problems, then it would be difficult to say that it is particularly good. The specific details of such a situation are very important, so I cannot say in general whether he should stay or he should leave. It varies in each case.

In fact, there are two pieces of advice in this text that come into play here and they may at first seem contradictory. One says do not abandon your enemies because they help you develop patience. The other one says abandon harmful companions because they obstruct Dharma. This is not a contradiction. Someone who is able to be patient with the aggression of others, especially in situations where it cannot be avoided, can use the aggression of others to further the practice of patience. If the aggression is too strong to be patient with and it impedes your practice of Dharma completely, then it is appropriate to remove yourself from such a situation.

As for the situation of the Tibetan refugees, many left during the invasion in order to be able to practice Dharma elsewhere, while some left simply to flee for their lives. In general, since that time, they have engaged in activities that correspond to their reason for leaving. Those who left in order to be able to practice Dharma have been practicing a lot of Dharma, and those who left simply to survive have done their best to survive and get rich if possible.

That is the general situation. As for what a specific person should do in the type of situation you describe, I cannot really say off hand.

Q: Does stable commitment mean that when I am practicing Hevajra I can never shift to Kalachakra? If I am chanting one mantra, how many times should I chant it before I shift to another one?

A: This depends upon the individual. Someone who has confidence or full knowledge and recognition that all deities embody the complete qualities and power of buddhahood need only practice one deity. It does not particularly matter which one it is, as long as it is a deity in which he or she has complete certainty. Someone who does not have that understanding, but sees things in a conceptual way and thinks that we need to practice one deity for attaining wealth, one deity for attaining enlightenment, one deity for forceful activity, one deity for pacification, and so forth, will have to practice different deities to attain these respective results. Someone who has the profound understanding that they are all the same will, by realizing one deity, realize all of them.

Q: I am asking this question for a friend who is practicing Pure Land Buddhism. He asks if there are any special methods in vajrayana leading to rebirth in Dewachen,[12] and exactly how many times we should chant the specific mantra to insure rebirth in Dewachen?

A: There is a difference between the sutra and the tantric presentations of Amitabha practice in the methods that are applied. The root of them both and the intention of them both is the same—obtaining rebirth in Dewachen, the pure land. The main difference is that in the context of sutra practice we consider ourselves as ordinary beings and we maintain our ordinary conception of the body, speech, and mind. We recognize the presence of Amitabha in the midst of his pure realm and we supplicate him. This is somewhat like someone who is in prison supplicating a powerful individual outside to do everything possible to get him or her out of prison. That is basically the sutra approach.

In the tantric approach, the supplication to Amitabha is exactly the same, but instead of just bringing to mind the fact that Amitabha is there in Dewachen, we actually visualize the realm of Dewachen, including Amitabha, in front of us as though he were actually present in our experience. Also, we do not consider ourselves to be ordinary, but we consecrate our body as a deity, our speech as mantra, and so forth. Continuing with the above analogy, it is as though in order to become free from our imprisonment, we not only appeal to someone outside who can release us from prison, but we also develop the power in ourselves that enables us to break out.

The reason for this difference in approach is the view. One aspect of the view of vajrayana is that all of the bodies and realms of buddhas such as Amitabha are spontaneously present in our minds already. We can experience them externally only because of their spontaneous presence within us, and this type of liberation can occur through the meeting of the internal and external conditions. For example, the sun is something physically external to us, but to see sunlight we must have eyes, and our eyes must be open. In the same way, liberation into the realm of Sukhavati is considered from the vajrayana point of view to be accomplished through the interdependence of external and internal conditions. As far as the recitation of mantras, there are different mantras used in different practices associated with this cycle. It would not really be possible to say that we have to recite a particular number in order to attain rebirth in Dewachen.

Q: How do we know we are suitable for mahayana or vajrayana practice? Is the vajrayana practice very dangerous? If we break the vows will we to fall into vajra hell?

A: In general, people meet the type of teachers, among those who teach the different vehicles, that accord with their own disposition and the extent of their own merit. As for what it is appropriate for individuals to practice among the various vehicles, they should practice what those teachers to whom they naturally become connected emphasize, and they should teach what is in accord with their own confidence and their own insight into the Dharma. This is not only true with respect to the mahayana and vajrayana, it is true with all levels of Buddhist teachings—hinayana, mahayana, vajrayana, and so forth. Basically, you should practice what you can, what naturally appeals to you, and what your inclination is toward. The main thing is your interest and confidence in the teachings, so you should practice whatever teachings you have the most confidence in.

As for the danger of vajrayana, it is true that vajrayana has great efficacy and can also be dangerous. The vajrayana presents a path for people with great insight who are able to be very careful and methodical in their practice. It presents a path by which such persons can, using the excellent methods of vajrayana, attain awakening in a very effective manner. It is true that if someone does not have this kind of insight, is not diligent, and especially lacks faith and devotion, she or he might violate the samaya, the commitments of vajrayana.

Practically speaking, though, we must make a distinction between two types of empowerment, since it is at empowerment that samaya are taken on. We can distinguish between an empowerment that is a blessing and what is called the ultimate or actual empowerment. Through faith and interest in a lama, you may receive from him or her a blessing empowerment that involves various substances, vases, and so forth being placed on your head and mantras recited to you. The function of this is to plant a seed for your future liberation, based upon the empowerment process and your own openness or faith in it. Such processes and methods are a special characteristic and quality of vajrayana and are very beneficial for the individuals involved. We must distinguish between that and the ultimate empowerment, in which a student, at the time of receiving the empowerment, generates the wisdom associated with the empowerment through a complete understanding of everything that is occurring. If someone were to receive the ultimate empowerment and then not make any use of it and not practice, but just be involved in mundane activities and turn his or her back on Dharma, then such a person could certainly break samaya.

There is, of course, still samaya with the empowerment as blessing, the common form of empowerment. However, when people take these empowerments, by and large they do not understand everything about what is going on. They do not understand exactly what is to be practiced and what is to be rejected, and they are just committing themselves perhaps to reciting the mantra, visualizing the deity, and so forth. Practically speaking, it is unlikely that people in such situations will harm themselves with vajrayana.

Q: Could you explain the difference between an ordinary vow and samaya?

A: Vow, or *dompa* in Tibetan, and samaya, or *damtsig*, are basically different terms for much the same thing. Generally speaking, the term *dompa*, which is usually translated as vow, is used in discussions of sutra, and the term *damtsig* or samaya is used in the context of tantra. The term *dompa* means "that which binds," in the sense of protecting us from the loss or impairment of the qualities of the path that we have acquired, and protecting us from the entrance of obstacles from the outside—so it keeps in and it keeps out. A metaphor for this is a belt. The function of binding yourself with a belt is to prevent you from losing your clothing. For example, if you think of the belt that holds a *chuba* shut, it prevents the chuba from falling open and whatever you are holding in the chuba from falling out; but it also protects your body from the wind and sun and so forth by holding the chuba closed. Vows or *dompa* are like that. They bind, and by binding, they protect. This term is basically one that is used in the sutras or is common to both sutra and tantra.

The term used most often in tantra is *damtsig*, which literally means "binding word" or "command." The analogy here is the command of a king, the disobeying of which would mean certain death. The emphasis here is on the danger of ignoring the prescriptions and proscriptions of samaya, but the danger does not come from the fear of punishment as it does with a king, but because samaya is a natural expression of the quality of the vajrayana Dharma. It is not an arbitrary command imposed on us; it is simply the rules that must be followed for the qualities not to turn into defects. For example, if you are traveling in an automobile there are certain rules you must follow to avoid killing yourself. If you are traveling in an airplane there are more rules because the qualities and the efficacy of the vehicle are greater. If you jump out of an airplane you are dead, and if you jump out of vajrayana, you are in vajra hell. The strictness or the ferocity of the samaya is directly proportional to the qualities of the vajrayana.

Q: The tenth point under the ten things that are necessary to practice Dharma was the application of insight or knowledge that does not have the "defect of reification." I do not really understand what the defect of reification means, and I would be interested in knowing more about what we can do to avoid it.

A: First of all, the root text from which this explanation is derived has the statement, "It is necessary that our view of all things not stray into reification or the false imputation of solidity and inherently present characteristics; and we avoid this by means of knowledge, understanding, and realization." This means that with respect to everything we experience, we must transcend ego-clinging, or more precisely, the false imputation of an inherently existent self and the false imputation of solidity or reality to our experiences. This is true not only with things in general, but also with our attitude toward Dharma and Dharma practice. When we are meditating on a deity, if we fixate on the solidity of that meditation and regard the deity as something with an external physical existence, a flesh and blood body that looks like that particular deity, then there is a mistake. That view will not lead to realization. If there is a fixation on the characteristics or form of the deity as being anything other than an expression of the wisdom that the deity embodies, it will not lead to the realization to which the practice should lead. It is the same when we are considering pure realms. If we think that a buddha realm is something that exists in a specific place and is made of solid objects with such and such form, like the world we experience, if we fixate on an imputed solidity and imputed characteristics of that realm, this will not lead to liberation into that realm because it simply perpetuates our ordinary manner of experience.

It is said that the form of the deity, and therefore the form of the realm of that deity, is a body of light the essence of which is wisdom. Light here does not mean physical light; it means a presence that is totally insubstantial. The deity having an essence of wisdom means that the form is merely the embodiment of the wisdom, efficacy, and activity for the benefit of beings that is the deity. Therefore, it is said that the form of the deity is like rays of rainbow light, and the essence of the deity is wisdom itself. Ultimately, however, this statement refers to the fact that our final understanding must be the realization of emptiness that is totally without any kind of elaboration, any kind of realizer and realization, any kind of intellectual attitude or position whatsoever. Thus the final point is to transcend conceptual mind.

6 The Ten Things to Be Known

Next comes the ten things that are to be known or understood. Whereas the previous set of "things not to be abandoned" have to be put into practice, these are things that merely have to be understood.

The first thing to understand is that external appearances are the manifestation of our confusion. We should recognize that the way we experience the world is without any inherent validity or inherent truth. The way we experience the world is based on ego-clinging, the false imputation of an inherently existent self. We therefore impute a truth or reality to our experience of the world that is equally false, because the way we experience things is simply the display of our minds. If we recognize that, our experiences are self-liberating. There is no fixation on what we experience. The way we experience the world is like seeing the reflection of the moon in a body of water. It is no more valid to say that what we experience has objective reality than it is valid to say that the reflection of the moon is another moon—that there is one moon in the sky and another in the water. This is valid to the degree that it is an experience, but it is not the moon itself; it is a reflection of the moon.

We experience things the way we do because of our habits, because of the influence of our past actions. Recognizing this is called recognizing the hidden evil or deception in the way we experience appearances. To illustrate the difference between recognizing this and not, suppose someone says that outside of this country, beyond a certain range of mountains, there is a magnificent realm full of delightful things. If you have not seen it, you cannot possibly conceive of it because you have no personal experience of it. It is just something you have heard. You might believe it or you might not, but you really have no definitive idea of it. Someone who has been there would know. In the same way, when you recognize the fact that the way you experience the world has no inherent validity beyond simply being your experience, then your fixation diminishes.

The second point is that, since the mind in itself (which is considered to be internal, as opposed to external appearances) has no inherent existence, it should be known to be empty. By recognizing the emptiness or lack of inherent existence of the mind, three types of fixations can be dispelled. These are fixation on the mind as a self, fixation on the mind as something real, and fixation on the mind as something solid.

The third point is that thoughts arise merely from the coming together of a variety of conditions, and should therefore be recognized as being adventitious, which means suddenly appearing and disappearing and not inherent to the nature of the mind. This recognition is important, because if we believe that thoughts are real and solid, then the fixation on thoughts produced by that misconception leads to the accumulation of karma through the power of the thoughts.

The fourth thing to be understood is that this body and speech that are produced from the elements are composite things. They are not unitary things and therefore they are impermanent. By recognizing the impermanence and composite nature of our body and speech, the tendency to fixate on them as permanent and solid things is dispelled.

The fifth thing to be known is that all of the various experiences of pleasure and suffering that are undergone by the various types of sentient beings arise from karma, from the previous actions of those particular beings. Therefore, it should be understood that the results of actions are infallible—what you do will have a certain result that will be experienced by you. What you experience is definitely a result of your own previous actions.

The sixth point is that suffering and sickness are a cause of stable renunciation for a practitioner of Dharma, and therefore should be understood to be a kind and valuable teacher. First of all, the experience of sickness and suffering by a practitioner is a cause of his or her future happiness, because this experience of suffering, if it is undergone with awareness, will exhaust the karma that produced it. If this sickness were not experienced now, and the karma ripened later, it would ripen as a much more intense experience of suffering lasting for a much longer period of time. Furthermore, sickness and suffering exhort the practitioner to renunciation because they show that there is negative karma. Therefore, as a practitioner, you should rejoice in the present experience of suffering, and also use it to further your renunciation by recognizing that it means you still have karma that could lead to tremendous future suffering.

The seventh point is that since attachment to pleasure and happiness is the root of samsara, we should know this attachment to be the *devaputra-mara,* or *lhai bu'i du* in Tibetan—the demon that is the child of the gods.[13] The experiences of the three realms of samsara[14] arise from clinging to or fixating on the experience of pleasure and trying to acquire it. Intoxication with this experience of pleasure is the cause of the sufferings of samsara. Therefore this type of experience should be recognized as the devaputra-mara.

The eighth point is that since distractions and entertainments are impediments to the accumulation of merit, they should be understood to be obstacles to the practice of Dharma. If we devote our time to meaningless distractions and entertainments, this is a form of procrastination in our practice. It interrupts our practice so that it takes a much longer time to get anything done. This steals away our accumulation of merit, and therefore should be understood to be something we must avoid.

The ninth thing to understand is that the obstacles to practice that come about through suddenly arising circumstances or conditions, such as aggressive action by others, sickness, and so forth, are exhortations to the cultivation of virtue. Therefore, those enemies and obstructers should be known to be our teachers, our lamas. As was said before, if we can meet adverse conditions with the further development of love and compassion for others—specifically, with the attitude that "whatever sufferings similar to mine other sentient beings have to go through, may only I have to go through them"—then the adverse conditions actually foster the practice of Dharma. In particular, when other people are being aggressive to you, from their point of view it may seem to be aggression. But if you look at its ultimate effect on you as a practitioner, it is a little like someone saying to you, "If you don't get out of samsara, this is the kind of stuff you will have to deal with again and again." It is an exhortation to renunciation and an exhortation to practice. Thus from your own point of view, from their ultimate effect on you, aggressive people are really your teachers.

The tenth point is that since all things have no inherent nature, we should know that all things, without any exception whatsoever, are in their nature the same, and that their nature is that sameness. Ordinarily, in the experience of people without the realization of the ultimate nature, there is a great deal of difference between *things*, on the one hand, which are distinct from each other, and, on the other hand, the *nature* of all things, which is the same. This nature is the lack of an essence to their characteristics. However, when this nature itself is recognized, it is seen that there is no difference between things and their nature. The conventional and the absolute are the same, because any thing is the expression of its nature, and the nature of every thing is the same. Therefore, since every thing expresses the same nature, every thing in its nature is the same.

That is what is to be understood here. This tenth thing to be understood is primarily directed toward experienced practitioners who have some realization, and for them it is something not merely to be understood but to be practiced and realized. For beginners, it is something to be understood as a concept or an idea.

These are the ten things to be known or understood. The understanding of such things that is arrived at through inferential reasoning, in the context of study and reflection, is quite different from the direct realization of their meaning, which can only come through meditation practice. Understanding alone is not a sufficient basis for moral decisions, for deciding what to accept and what to abandon. We should know the difference between a conceptual recognition and a definitive attainment of realization.

7 The Ten Things to Be Practiced

The previous list was ten things to be known, and next come ten things we should actually practice. The first is, having entered into the door of Dharma, do not engage in the herd-like behavior of meaningless human activity, but practice Dharma properly. Once we have begun the practice of Dharma, it is important to rely upon the appropriate conditions that will support our beginning practice of Dharma, such as staying in a solitary environment where practice is possible, and surrounding ourselves with companions who will help us. We must not allow ourselves to be drawn into a lot of meaningless and distracting activities. This can happen very easily in the beginning, and it prevents us from making full use of our entrance into Dharma practice. It is important, from the very beginning of our practice until the day of our death, to make full use of the opportunity of Dharma by providing ourselves with conditions that support the practice, such as environment, companions, and so forth.

The second thing to be practiced is, having abandoned your birthplace, do not establish yourself too firmly in any one place. In other words, practice without attachment. As was said before, it is important to abandon your birthplace, the place to which you are most attached, with the correct aspiration of wishing to transcend the attachment of samsara. You might leave the place of your birth, but if you do not give up attachment, you will recreate the attachments associated with your birthplace in some other place. You will identify with a specific environment and settle into it, and that is no better than being attached to your birthplace. It is important, no matter where you are, to preserve a lack of attachment.

The third thing to be practiced is, relying upon an authentic guru, abandon arrogance, and practice in accordance with his or her command. In relying upon a teacher, you must respect the validity of his or her teachings and instructions, and not have the kind of arrogant attitude that makes you think inside that you know better. It is said that qualities cannot come to rest on the hard iron ball of arrogance. People often have the attitude that, "My teachers know a lot about Dharma, but I would not take their advice about mundane things. When it comes to really serious decisions, I do not trust them so much." If you have such a strong distrust of your gurus, which comes from a kind of arrogance, there is no possibility of your generating their qualities and developing the kind of compassion they embody.

The fourth thing to be practiced is, having trained your mind through hearing and contemplation, or through study and analysis, do not just be involved in talking about it, but actually put what you have understood into practice. Receiving instructions or coming to an understanding and merely repeating it to others will not do you any good. All it does is create echoes. When you are hungry and you have food, you will only relieve your hunger to the extent that you actually eat. The whole point of having food is for it to be consumed in order to relieve someone's hunger. In the same way, you must actually put into practice and make use of any instruction you receive and anything you come to understand through analysis.

The fifth thing to be practiced is that if experience or realization is generated in your mental continuum, do not be satisfied with that, but continue practicing without distraction. It is often possible to have some kind of experience or slight realization and think that this is enough, that further diligence and practice are unnecessary. That is mistaken. It is like trying to rub two pieces of wood together to make fire, and when they start to smoke, thinking that this is enough. The smoke is an indication that if you keep on rubbing, you will get a fire, but smoke itself is not a fire; smoke itself is not enough. The indications of successful practice that you experience are not indications that you have no need to practice further; they are indications that if you practice even more diligently, you will reach some result or fruition. Therefore, experience and realization should spur you to further effort and not to abandoning effort.

The sixth thing to be practiced is that when practice has, to some extent, entered into your mental continuum, do not enter into meaningless distractions in the midst of many people, but continue the practice. For example, after you have finished a period of retreat, if you enter into a state of complete distraction and waste a lot of time, then as time goes on, the benefit you have received from the practice, the indications of a successful practice, and the changes in your personality that are marks of practice, will decrease, and your distraction and mindlessness will increase. Finally, if you do not turn away from that direction, you will find that there is not the slightest mark of any kind of benefit left from the practice you have done. The point is that if you practice, you have to keep on practicing. You cannot stop and just be careless.

The seventh thing to be practiced is, having committed yourself to undertake a certain discipline and mode of conduct in the presence of the *khenpo*, or *upadyaya*, or preceptor in the case of *vinaya*, or the vajra master in the case of samaya, do not let your three gates—your body, speech, and mind—slip into carelessness and laziness, but continually practice the three trainings in accordance with the commitments you have made. The three trainings are personal discipline or morality, meditation, and the acquisition of knowledge and understanding.

The eighth thing to be practiced is, having generated bodhicitta—the intention to attain supreme awakening—do not practice merely for your own benefit, but perform all activities, and especially all practice, for the benefit of others. In connection with this, many people come to me and say, "I cannot take the bodhisattva vow, because I am really mostly concerned about myself. I cannot just abandon that in one instant and pretend that I am concerned only about other people." In a certain way this is a valid remark, but when you take the bodhisattva vow it is not the case that you must immediately, in an instant, become perfect. You have to keep on working, or doing whatever you need to do to survive, but you should practice as much Dharma as you can, and practice it for the benefit of others. Slowly, by instilling that motivation, the concern for others will grow and the training connected with the bodhisattva vow will take root in you.

The ninth thing to be practiced is, having entered into the door of secret mantra through receiving empowerment, do not leave your body, speech, and mind in a state of ordinariness, but practice maintaining your body, speech, and mind as the three mandalas. This means recognizing that your body is the deity, that speech and all sound are mantra, and that whatever occurs in the mind is the expanse of wisdom. The point of this is to maintain the attitude that your body, speech, and mind are the body, speech, and mind of all buddhas.

Then the tenth thing to be practiced is, when you are young, do not waste your time wandering around meaninglessly, but practice with austerity in the presence of authentic teachers. When people are young they tend to go sightseeing, to run around and experiment a bit. For example, in Tibet, when people were young they would often spend a lot of time going on pilgrimage to the eighteen regions and so forth. It is true that these are places that have great blessings because they have been consecrated by the siddhas of the past, but going to the various mountains and so forth involves quite a bit of difficulty and hardship. It would be better, when you are young and have a clear mind and a strong body, to make use of these faculties, not in such activities, but by staying in one place and practicing in the presence of teachers, which involves much the same hardship.

These are the ten things to be practiced.

8 The Ten Things to Emphasize

Next are the ten things to emphasize, or the ten things to be diligent about. The first of these is, when you are a beginner, be diligent in hearing and contemplation, or study and analysis, because if you know absolutely nothing about the Dharma, you cannot practice; you have no idea what to practice or how to practice it. At the very beginning it is important to concentrate on acquiring the necessary information and making sure that you understand it.

The second thing to be diligent about is, having generated the experience and basic understanding that comes from acquiring information and analyzing it, emphasize the practice of meditation.

In the context of meditation practice, the third point is, until you attain stability, exert yourself in solitude. Stability means a stage in your practice in which your mind is not affected in any way by any kind of external conditions or circumstances whatsoever, and is not affected in any way by any kind of thought or emotion that can occur in the mind. Until you attain such a degree of stability, it is necessary to practice in solitude.

In the context of intense practice, the fourth point is, if you find that your mind wanders a lot and is constantly going out to objects, and if you find that you are prey to excitement or agitation of the mind, then be diligent in relaxing your awareness to pacify this agitation.

The fifth point is, if, on the other hand, you find that you are prey to torpor and mental fogginess, then uplift your awareness. This means, for example, straightening your posture and slightly intensifying the application of awareness. Of the two defects that are mentioned here, the first one, *jingwa,* which means sunkenness or torpor, is a state of physical and mental depression or sleepiness—not necessarily emotional depression—and the second one, *mukpa,* or mental fogginess, is a lack of mental clarity.

The sixth point is, until your mind becomes stable, emphasize even placement. The mind being stable refers to the state in which the mind is not affected by thoughts, the state in which the mind can direct itself to an object without there being any kind of hindrance from arising thoughts. Until you arrive at that stage, you should concentrate on even placement, which in this case means the practice of tranquility meditation or shamata.

The seventh point is, when you have become stable in even placement, then emphasize post-meditation. Post-meditation here does not mean not practicing. It means the class of formal practices that are done in order to accumulate merit, practices that are more structured than basic shamata or tranquility meditation. The point here is that when we have gained some tranquility, we should then apply that to the accumulation of merit, in order that our practice of tranquility does not merely become the absorption of the formless realms.

The eighth point is, if there seem to be many adverse conditions, then concentrate on and apply diligently the three types of patience. When things are not going well with any aspect of your practice or your life, you should apply the appropriate type of patience, rather than attempting to flee from the circumstances.

The first type of patience is called the patience that is the acceptance of suffering. This means accepting the experience of suffering you are undergoing, and not attempting to flee from it or deny it, but working with it directly. The second type is the patience that is certainty about the Dharma. This means being patient with the profundity of Dharma, which may not be very easy to understand, and being patient with the process of growing to understand it. The third type is, literally, "the patience that does not think anything whatsoever," but it means the patience of not making a big deal out of things. This refers to situations in which someone else is aggressive to you, and it means not reacting by scheming; not thinking, "So-and-so has done (or said) this, what should I do (or say) back?" and not working out strategies and complicated maneuvers, but just thinking, "Well, it is not a big deal, I do not have to do anything about it."

The ninth point is, if you have a great attachment and fixation on something, then forcefully or violently reverse that attachment. This means to concentrate on transcending whatever particular form of attachment torments you the most. In the case of a Kadampa teacher of the past, for example, there was a time when someone came begging food from him, and of course food meant roasted barley flour or *tsampa*. He did not have very much tsampa, and he was originally just going to give this person a handful because, when he looked at what he had, he thought that was all he could spare. Then he realized that he was very attached to this food and to measuring it out like that, so he gave the beggar everything he had, just to be able to cut through that miserliness.

Finally, if you find that you do not have very much loving-kindness and compassion, then concentrate upon developing bodhicitta. You should carefully consider the benefits of bodhicitta, since it is the only possible cause of buddhahood, and the defects of not possessing bodhicitta, since without it there is no possibility of awakening. Therefore, consider the need to engage in the process of developing loving-kindness and compassion. Reason with yourself and analyze the situation. Come to an understanding that no matter how it may seem, the root of all suffering is in actuality the desire to accomplish our own benefit and our own aims, and the root of all happiness is the relinquishment of that concern and the desire to accomplish the benefit of others. Having understood these things as they are explained in the mahayana texts, then cultivate them as best you can.

These are the ten things to be done diligently, or ten things to emphasize in specific situations.

9 The Ten Exhortations

Next come the ten things that are exhortations. The first of these is, thinking of the difficulty of obtaining the freedom and resources of the precious human existence, exhort yourself to practice the holy Dharma. Consider that the only possible basis for the attainment of the precious human existence is having accumulated an inconceivable amount of merit over an inconceivably long period of time, and therefore it is very, very hard to attain it, and very unlikely that we could attain it without the intentional effort to do so through the cultivation of virtue. Consideration of this exhorts us to the practice of Dharma.

Second, thinking of death and impermanence, exhort yourself to practice virtue. Consider further that this precious human existence that we now possess, which is so rare, does not last very long, and therefore there is no time to waste. If we wish to make use of it and if we wish to attain it again, we must practice as much virtue as possible. These considerations lead to actually engaging in practice.

Third, thinking of the infallibility of the results of action, exhort yourself to abandon wrongdoing. Consider that a harmful action not only harms others but also harms you, because it yields an unpleasant result in the future experience of the doer of the action, and that a virtuous action not only helps others but will definitely help you in the future. If you consider this and have confidence in this, you will naturally avoid whatever is harmful.

Fourth, considering the defects of samsara, exhort yourself to the attainment of liberation. Consider that no matter which one of the six states of existence[15] you are born in, it is an experience that is entirely made up of the three types of suffering.[16] Through actually thinking about how bad samsara is, you will naturally develop the motivation to be liberated from that state of existence, and you will actually engage in the methods that lead to liberation.

Fifth, thinking that you are not alone in your suffering, that all sentient beings within samsara undergo terrible suffering, exhort yourself to cultivate bodhicitta.

Sixth, thinking that the attitudes of all sentient beings are incorrect or mistaken, exhort yourself to be diligent in hearing and contemplation. By recognizing the fact that the way we all view our experience is mistaken or inaccurate, you recognize the need to study, and to analyze the information that is acquired through study.

Seventh, thinking of how difficult it is to uproot the habit of confusion that we have cultivated during a period a time that has no beginning, exhort yourself to practice meditation.

Eighth, thinking that in these degenerate times the mental afflictions become stronger and stronger, exhort yourself to apply the particular remedy or antidote for each one.

Ninth, thinking that there are many adverse conditions in these degenerate times that we live in, exhort yourself to apply patience. It is said that patience is especially necessary in bad or degenerate times because there are so many adverse conditions that increase the instances of people harming each other. Thus it becomes more and more necessary to cultivate patience, which is said to be the most important Dharma quality to have in such circumstances.

Tenth, thinking that constant distraction will waste your entire human life, exhort yourself to be diligent.

These are the ten things to use as exhortations.

10 The Ten Deviations

Next are the ten deviations. The first of these is, if you have little faith but are very intelligent, you may deviate into becoming a big talker. If you understand the Dharma intellectually, but, not having much faith, you do not really practice it, then your approach becomes a lot of words.

The second deviation is that if, on the other hand, you have a great deal of faith but not much insight, then you will stray into solidifying everything and blindly going forward, or working really hard without knowing what you are doing. This means that you will not have any recognition of the meaning of what you are practicing, so you will not actually be able to attain the realization that the practice should lead to.

Third, if you are very diligent, but lack instruction, you will deviate into practice with defects and mistakes. You may be very diligent in your practice but not receive instruction from qualified teachers that includes advice such as, "when you do this, this may happen, and if that happens then you should do that; if this experience arises, then do not worry about it, it just means you should do this," and so forth. If you lack such instruction, you will be deceived by your own experiences, and you will stray into deception and downfall.

Fourth, if you have not previously cut through misconceptions through study and analysis, or hearing and contemplation, then the practice of meditation will simply be the cultivation of the state of mental darkness or stupidity. This could be like just sitting there and trying not to think, just closing up and closing in.

Fifth, if you do not immediately put into practice your understanding of Dharma, you will become a jaded scholar. When you come to an understanding of something or receive some practical instructions, if you do not make use of it immediately, the desire to make use of it becomes less and less over time. You become more and more jaded and start to think less and less of the value of Dharma and the instructions you have received. You keep on receiving more and more instructions and acquiring more and more knowledge or information, but it remains just as information, and you have less and less desire to practice. On the other hand, if you immediately put into practice instructions you receive, your desire to practice them increases. The more practice you do, the more your respect for the instructions and your understanding of their true value will increase.

Sixth, if you do not train yourself in the aspect of method, which is the cultivation of compassion, then, having concern only for your own benefit and your own liberation, you will stray into the lesser vehicle. This means that if you do not generate a pure intention to accomplish the benefit of others through having compassion and genuine concern for their benefit, then no matter what practice you do, it will still be the lower vehicle, because it is the motivation that separates these.

Even if you are practicing secret mantra, which is certainly the greater vehicle, and you are doing *pujas*, visualizing deities, reciting mantras, and so forth, if you have no compassion, then it is not really secret mantra at all. That situation is a little bit like someone who has a very powerful gun that could shoot a bullet very accurately over a long distance, but who fires it pointed down at the ground. Thus it is essential to have a commitment to the benefit of others, and to understand the importance of emphasizing the benefit of others in your motivation for practice.

Seventh, if you do not train your mind in the aspect of knowledge, which is the correct understanding of emptiness, whatever you practice will simply be the cultivation of further samsara. If you do not come to an understanding of emptiness, then whatever you do has ego-clinging and a persistent belief in your own inherent existence as its basic motivation or starting point. With that as a basis, no matter what you practice, whether it is the most profound secret mantra or anything else, it will only be the further cultivation of ego.

Eighth, if you do not transcend or defeat the eight worldly dharmas, then whatever practice you do will only be a mundane ornament. If the motivation for your practice is the wish to acquire possessions, fame, respect, and service, and the fear that these will diminish, then Dharma practice will lead to a slight acquisition of such things, which is like a pretty, meaningless ornament, but it will not lead to anything else.

Ninth, if people in villages get too interested in you and have too much faith in you, then you can stray into becoming someone who just attends to the wishes of other people. This point is expressed in terms of a situation that might arise in Tibet: if you are a practitioner and let villagers have too much faith and interest in you, you will just become a slave to popularity. It means that if you cater too much to the attention of other people, then that is where your mind will be, and your practice will degenerate into simply trying to please them.

Tenth, if you have generated some qualities and some personal power through your practice, but your mind is not stable—you have some kind of qualities while you practice, but you do not have the stability or maturity that would enable you to remain in solitude and just concentrate on practice—then you may become someone who wanders around villages doing little pujas to please the people and acquire offerings.

These are the ten types of deviation.

QUESTIONS AND ANSWERS

Q: It was said that suffering and sicknesses are good teachers. Should we then stop having compassion for those people who suffer and have sicknesses?

A: It is necessary to have compassion when other people are suffering and sick because, from your own point of view, the aspiration of looking at the suffering of others, and wishing that their suffering could be absorbed into your suffering so they would not have to go through it, is the basis for the development and path of bodhicitta. As far as your own suffering is concerned, you should view that as a demonstration of the results of negative actions, and this will inspire you to avoid wrongdoing and cultivate virtue. But with regard to the suffering of others, it is important to have the strong intention to do everything you can to alleviate their suffering. If you actually have the ability to do this physically, you should do so. If not, you should aspire to develop the ability to alleviate the suffering of all beings, and dedicate the virtue and merit of whatever practice you do—whatever mantras you recite or meditations you perform and so forth—to the alleviation of the suffering of all beings, and in particular, those beings you come in contact with who are manifestly suffering. When you see sick or suffering people, you should not think, "Well, that is a good teacher for them. I am glad they had that," because this attitude is only helpful when it is applied toward your own experiences, not toward those of others.

Q: Concerning the different stages of dealing with aggression, it seems that the teachings you have been giving are basically saying to give up attachments and the eight worldly dharmas—fame, respect, wealth, gain, and loss. In that context I am wondering, if you have faith in the teachers and you have faith in the practice, although you have not had much experience yourself, would the idea be just, in some sense, to give up and not really care what anybody says, just as long as you keep practicing and maintain your relationship with your gurus?

A: Yes.

Q: In this day and age people will say this is crazy.

A: If you have a stable confidence in the Dharma, you can just forget about the aggression of others, because the third kind of patience, the patience that is not making a big deal out of other's aggressions, consists of just that—not thinking anything of it.

Q: Just let it go and not worry about the consequences?

A: If you are a practitioner, you do not need to think about it at all. You do not need to worry about the future consequences, you do not have to try and figure out or imagine what their motivation might be, or anything like that. You just forget about it.

Q: So you just do your practice and keep your motivation as pure as you can?

A: Yes, you only have to worry about your own motivation and not that of others, because if you start to think about what other people's motivations are, you might not be able to determine them. Also, if you try to correct their motivation or way of looking at things, while it is possible that you might be able to help, it is more likely that you will just strengthen their mental afflictions.

Q: You spoke about dealing with your mind in different ways according to different *yanas* or vehicles. In the hinayana you try to cut your own suffering, in the mahayana you realize that other people are suffering and you try to do things for the benefit of others, and then in the vajrayana you see your mind as the dharmakaya or wisdom. When you go though this process, do you sort of grind your mind down through the techniques of first two yanas, so that by the time you become a vajrayana practitioner you can see your mind in that way, and you have more space around you for your thoughts? Do your thoughts change, or do they remain essentially the same in nature, so it is just the way you are working with them when they arise that is different?

A: The gradation of approaches corresponding to the different vehicles is as you said. As for the situation of a vajrayana practitioner, there are two types of vajrayana practitioners, a vajrayana practitioner in name and an actual vajrayana practitioner. When we begin to practice vajrayana we are just vajrayana practitioners in name. We do not have any vajrayana level of realization; that has to come through practice. An authentic or actual practitioner of vajrayana is someone who has actually attained the realizations corresponding to the previous vehicles and generated the qualities that those vehicles embody, and who is starting to develop the qualities of the vajrayana path as well. Then it is like having wings—he or she transcends a lot of nonsense. However, thoughts do not cease for an authentic vajrayana practitioner. Such a practitioner sees the nature of thoughts to be self-liberated and sees that they cannot possibly harm his or her realization. It is said that there is no need to cause thoughts to cease, and it is also impossible.

However, in the case of an *arya* practitioner (someone who has attained at least the first bodhisattva level, or *bhumi*) we have to distinguish the presence or absence of thought according to whether he or she is engaged in even-placement meditation or in post-meditation. In meditation, a bodhisattva has no thoughts and in post-meditation he or she has thoughts, yet recognizes their nature. At the time of fruition, when one attains complete buddhahood, there are no thoughts.

Q: So is the path in vajrayana recognizing the nature of thoughts each time they arise?

A: That would be very good, but it also would be very difficult. Basically what is emphasized is, when a strong mental affliction or klesha arises, looking directly at the essence or nature of that mental affliction, and seeing it to be self-liberated. It is not so much any thought, but a strong mental affliction, that is treated in this manner.

Q: This question has to do with mental fixation. In general it appears from the teachings that any conceptual idea about the world is mental fixation. But in the practice of meditation, when the mind becomes fixated on the same distracting thought over and over again, is the way to work with that fixation just continually to look at that as thinking, and then gradually it becomes released from its conceptual nature?

For example, when I am trying to visualize Chenrezig, at certain times the same thought intrudes again and again, like a broken record. After a while I realize, "This is thinking." I keep coming back to the visualization, but the more I try, the more the thoughts keep arising.

A: Well, that is what training in the generation stage is like. In the beginning you generate a visualization, and then you become distracted, and then you return to the visualization, and then again you become distracted, and you return, and so forth. That experience arises for everyone at the beginning of this kind of training. To deal with this, various methods or approaches to visualization are presented, in order that the practitioner can avoid this broken record syndrome.

For example, let us say you are visualizing a deity in front of you in space. At times you direct your attention to the presence of the deity and to the whole form, and at other times you go through the details of the appearance, starting from the top of the head down to the bottom, and then from the bottom up to the top, and so forth. Through such methods, eventually your mind starts to become trained and tamed in the context of that visualization, and then it will come to rest more on the visualization. Until you become trained, you will still have to go through the experience of becoming distracted and returning to the technique, which is in this case the visualization.

When starting to visualize deities, often people have the experience of forgetting, in the most basic sense of that word, what the deity looks like, having actually to try to remember what they are wearing, what their ornaments are, and so forth. In order to train people there are additional visualizations, such as the projection and withdrawal of rays of light, as well as various ways of clarifying the visualization of the deity's form, such as starting from the inside and moving out, or starting from the outside and moving in. There are also more complex visualizations, for example, one in which rays of light are projected from the deity's heart and make offerings to all buddhas and bodhisattvas, and then the rays of light are drawn back in, and go out again and transform all sentient beings into the deity, purifying their obscurations. The function of all of these is to enable the practitioner to bring the mind to rest within the framework of the visualization.

Q: I have a question on the view of emptiness. Is *shentong* the ultimate view of emptiness? Also, I remember that you said once in the teachings on *The Profound Inner Meaning*[17] that trees do not have sentience, but some Buddhists who have studied the *Avatamsaka Sutra* say that every object has sentience. What are the correct views of sentience and emptiness?

A: There are evidently different interpretations of the words of the sutras. Sections of the *Avatamsaka Sutra* that might be construed elsewhere in the way you suggest, have traditionally not been construed that way in Tibet. From the sutra point of view, it is not considered that inanimate objects have awareness. From the point of view of tantra, the five elements of which inanimate objects are composed are in their nature the five female buddhas, the five consorts, and they are of the nature of wisdom. Thus, while it is not asserted in the sutras that inanimate objects have awareness, in the tantras it is said that everything is of the nature of wisdom.

With regard to whether or not the "empty of other" or *shentong* position is the final and ultimate statement of emptiness, generally speaking there are two aspects to determining the status of experienced things. When it is determined that the appearances that we experience have no inherent existence or nature, and are therefore empty of possessing their own individual nature that makes them what they are, then that is called "the determination of self-emptiness" or *rangtong*.

Further, when it is determined that emptiness, the nature that is the lack of inherent existence of all things, is not merely a total absence of anything, but is at the same time the spontaneous presence of all of the qualities of awakening—the bodies and realms of all buddhas—then, since the nature is empty of defilements that are other than itself, this is called "the empty of other determination" or the shentong approach. The two views are thus not particularly conflicting.

As for whether or not this type of approach is the ultimate one among the Buddha's teachings, there are many different assertions about which interpretation of the Buddha's words is the final or most profound one. From the point of view of the listeners and solitary realizers—the *shravakas* and *pratyekabuddhas*—the realization of the noninherent existence of the personal self is the final and ultimate meaning of the Buddha's teachings. Adhering to that position, they attain the state of an *arhat*. From the point of view of those who adhere to the Mind-only school, *that* is the ultimate position; and from the point of view of those who adhere to any of the Middle Way schools, *they* are the ultimate positions.

Therefore, I cannot say that the shentong view is the final one and is superior to the others. If you consider the view of secret mantra to be the highest view and the final destination of the Buddha's teachings, then it can be said that among the sutra views, it is the shentong view that comes closest to the view of secret mantra or vajrayana. In that sense it is useful because an understanding of the shentong view is a good way to gain access to the view of vajrayana. Rather than viewing one of these various presentations as ultimate and excluding others, it is more helpful from the vajrayana standpoint to view them as steps on a staircase.

11 The Ten Confusions of One Thing for Another

The next set of ten are the ten cases of confusing one thing for another. This refers to ten situations in which there are two attitudes that seem to be similar in appearance, but are very different in their effect and nature, and therefore are very easy to confuse for one another.

The first of these is that it is possible to confuse faith and desire. When you have faith in someone, that feels good; it is pleasant. When you are attached to someone personally, that also feels good. It is possible to confuse the one for the other in your attitude toward your teachers. Faith in teachers is appreciation of the fact that through their realization, their understanding, and their compassion, they teach the path that leads to liberation and omniscience. It is an interest in them and what they teach, a respect for them and for the process.

On the other hand, attachment, desire, or personal fixation on teachers is being attracted to them and taking delight in them because of their race, their appearance, the fact that they might be young, or something ephemeral or shallow in their personality.

Second, it is possible to mistake attachment for loving-kindness and compassion. Love and compassion are distinguished from attachment in that they apply equally to your friends and your enemies. Genuine love and compassion make no distinction based upon your relationship to the object of compassion. They are the wish that all sentient beings without exception have happiness and the causes of happiness, and the wish that all sentient beings without exception be free of suffering and the causes of suffering. The keynote of those two attitudes is that there is no hope involved of any kind of return or any sort of personal satisfaction as a result of the happiness of others.

In the case of attachment to someone, you wish that person well but it is based on an identification with him or her as "my friend, my son, my daughter." This identification and this feeling of ownership or territoriality is related to wanting some kind of return. You enjoy the happiness of that person because you have identified with him or her, and therefore in essence it is just wishing for your own benefit. Such attachment can very easily turn to aversion, anger, and hatred. That is the difference between compassion and attachment.

Third, it is possible to mix up the natural emptiness of all things with conceptually imputed emptiness. That is, we may confuse genuine emptiness with an idea of emptiness. Genuine emptiness, the actual nature of all things, is beyond any kind of elaboration, which means it is beyond any kind of conceptual description or conceptual appreciation. It cannot be encountered through thought. Therefore, when we think about emptiness and generate a concept or an idea of it, all we can do is negate aspects of our experience and call that negation emptiness. There is no direct experience of emptiness in such reasoning. Reasoning may be useful, but it cannot lead to a direct experience of the nature itself. It can only lead to a partial negation of misconceptions. Actual emptiness transcends not only existence or affirmation of existence, but also nonexistence or negation of existence. Emptiness is inconceivable and therefore must be distinguished from a conceptual idea of it.

Fourth, it is possible to mix up the expanse of qualities, the dharmadhatu, and the nihilistic view, the view of annihilation. Because the expanse of qualities is the nature of all things, it transcends being an interdependent thing. It is not brought about through causes and conditions. It is not a product and it is not a composite. This is quite different from the view that there is no interdependence and therefore no continuation of the results produced by our present and past actions. It is possible to confuse these two. Sometimes, when the nature of the dharmadhatu is presented, partial understanding of that nature may lead to the misunderstanding that there is no such thing as karma.

There was once an eminent teacher, a previous birth of Dodrupchen Rinpoche, who taught a course in which he set forth the view of the expanse of qualities. One of the monks attending the course misunderstood that view and thought it meant that there are no results to actions and that it was permissible to do anything. He went out and killed a goat. Then Dodrupchen Rinpoche asked him, "You are a Dharma person and a monk, how could you possibly kill a goat?" He replied, "You said that I do not exist, the goat does not exist, and the act of killing does not exist. Therefore, I thought there would be no problem." Dodrupchen Rinpoche was so agonized by the fact that his presentation had led to such a misunderstanding that he went into retreat and did not teach for years.

Fifth, it is possible to mix up experience and realization. A variety of experiences may arise within your practice which are indications that the practice is successful and is having some effect on you. Such experiences, such indications or signs are quite different from realization. Experiences by their nature decay and disappear, whereas realization does not and cannot disappear. If you fixate on an experience and direct your practice toward it, when the experience disappears you will be left with nothing, and certainly with no realization.

It is quite common for people to mistake these two. The difference is extreme because in realization all defects have been abandoned and the power of wisdom has expanded or blossomed. It is quite common for people who have some experiences while practicing to assume that they have attained realization. They assume that they are siddhas, and therefore they engage in conduct that they have heard is appropriate for siddhas. Then, of course, when they die they go to the lower realms.

Sixth, it is possible to mistake a good monk or nun for a phony. Good monks and nuns have abandoned that which is harmful to themselves and others, and they cultivate the mode of conduct prescribed in the vinaya or discipline. The way they should appear is also prescribed: there are certain robes that are worn a particular way, certain colors, certain implements that are held, certain things that are relinquished, and so forth. This is quite detailed, and a good monk or nun will maintain all of it. A phony would look the same on the outside, wearing the same robes, and would appear exactly the same in conduct, if you just looked at him or her. The difference is that a good monk or nun behaves the same way whether anyone is looking or not. He or she is the same in public and private. A phony is always very good when others are looking, but when no one is looking, is not so good.

Seventh, it is possible to confuse someone who, having manifestly realized the nature of all things, has eradicated all confusion, with someone who has been carried off by Mara and has gone berserk. When people have truly realized the nature of all things directly, finally, they have no fear. They are not afraid of anything. They have no hesitation. They have no personal needs; they do not care about themselves at all. Therefore, the way they might act is somewhat uncertain. We cannot say that they will act one way or another. On the other hand, the way a mad person—someone who has gone crazy because something has gone wrong with his or her practice—might act is equally uncertain. From our point of view we cannot really tell the difference.

Eighth, it is possible to confuse a siddha and a charlatan. Having completely realized the nature of all things and purified all defilements, siddhas do a variety of things for the benefit of sentient beings. For example, they might make predictions. Siddhas might say that twenty years from now such and such will happen. People find the actions of the siddhas quite useful and pleasing; it is helpful to know such things. Therefore, there are also charlatans who, seeing that people find siddhas very attractive, pretend to be siddhas and make predictions—saying that twenty years from now this and that will happen, and in the past certain things happened and so forth—in order to gain praise and get rich. Thus it is possible to confuse siddhas and charlatans.

Ninth, it is possible to confuse someone who is engaged in the benefit of others with someone who is engaged in his or her own benefit. Bodhisattvas and realized yogis will do anything they can to benefit sentient beings with their body, speech, and mind. They do a lot of good, and they dedicate all the merit they accumulate through the good they do to all sentient beings. They have no hope for any kind of personal result or personal gain through the good they do.

On the other hand, there are people who do a certain amount of good in order to attract a following and gain wealth and power. For example, there was once a Tibetan lama who went to Ladakh. He was not very well known, so he did not have very many followers and he did not receive very many offerings. Whatever offerings he received, though, he would use to offer butter lamps and make feast offerings and so forth in order to accumulate merit. When people heard about this, they were very much impressed with him; he was evidently the real thing, so they started making a lot of offerings to him. Huge numbers of people assembled around him—a whole city of students. In this way he accumulated a lot of money, at which point he went right back to Tibet. His use of the initial small offerings was a calculated investment. He knew that if it seemed that everything he offered was going toward meritorious projects, people would offer a lot more, at which point he could simply take the money.

Tenth, it is possible to confuse a skillful teacher with a deceptive or dishonest teacher. Skillful teachers do whatever they can and say whatever is necessary to enable people to enter into the practice of Dharma and to help their students avoid unnecessary difficulties and obstacles. A teacher who can do that is a very, very useful and excellent teacher. Genuine teachers of that type have no concern for any kind of benefit that will come to them. They have no fixation on what happens and no hopes with regard to their students' attitude towards them. On the other hand, there are people who act in somewhat similar ways, at least in appearance, but hide their own defects and pretend to have qualities they do not really possess. Using such deception, they manipulate people into accomplishing some kind of aim of their own such as the acquisition of wealth or followers, or both. It is possible to confuse these two kinds of teachers.

These are the ten situations in which two things look the same at first but are not in fact the same at all.

12 The Ten Unmistaken Things

Next are the ten things that are unmistaken. The first of these is, having no attachment to anything, to leave home, and having left home to have no home. This means to leave worldly life—to stop being a householder—and to have no attachment, that is, not try to make a home out of your ordination.

There are different ways in which a person might enter into a renunciate ordination. The really pure and correct approach is, having no attachment at all, not only to leave worldly life, but also to avoid recreating a nest or home in the ordination. But it is also possible for people to become ordained for social reasons, or become ordained in order to make a home for themselves, a secure situation in a monastery. While it is possible that they might eventually straighten out, their initial motivation is not correct.

Having generated such a genuine renunciation, the second thing that is unmistaken is to respect your teacher—the spiritual friend who is an authentic guru—so much that you carry him or her above your head like the cloth that binds your topknot. This refers to the practice of gathering the hair into a topknot, and in order for it not to unravel, putting a piece of white cotton around it. Now, we do not bind our topknots with cloth here in this country, but the point is to respect your teacher so much that you always imagine carrying him or her above your head.

Third, it is unmistaken to combine the three practices of hearing, contemplating, and meditating. Whenever you acquire Dharmic information through studying or receiving teachings, you should immediately investigate its meaning, analyze it until it is clear, and then apply it in your practice of meditation. You cannot meditate without having received the information, nor can you wait until you have totally perfected all learning before you begin practice. Therefore it is important to put into practice immediately everything you learn, after having analyzed it until you correctly understand it.

Fourth, it is unmistaken to have a high view and "low" conduct. This means that we should preserve the unexcelled view of the highest vehicle, the vajrayana, and practice this vehicle properly, but practice it within the context of the proper conduct that is indicated in the hinayana or lowest vehicle. We should conduct ourselves in accordance with the vinaya, wearing the appropriate robes and so forth. We should combine a profound understanding with careful conduct that is in accord with the vinaya.

Fifth, it is unmistaken to have a vast mind but a narrow commitment. In the manner of *kyebu dampa* or exalted individuals, the best way to do things is not to commit yourself to something too vast, not to talk too big in your commitment. If you make a tremendously large commitment in the beginning, you will not keep it up, and then your commitment will be like a design drawn in water. The best way to do things is to make a small commitment, stick to it, and never give it up until your death. Then gradually a lot is done. Keeping to a modest commitment is like carving something in stone. Someone who carves *mani* stones,[18] for example, will think of one at a time while doing the carving; but if he or she keeps on doing it for a long time, eventually a tremendous number of them will be done. Even though it is a small project at any given point, it adds up to something very significant over time.

Sixth, in the context of hearing and contemplation, it is unmistaken to have great insight and little pride. It is important to apply all the insight we can bring to bear on the processes of hearing and contemplation, but to do so without arrogance.

Seventh, in the context of practice, it is important to be rich in instruction and persevering in application. This means to receive a variety of instructions and to persevere and prolong the application of whatever particular practice we are engaged in.

Eighth, again in the context of practice, it is unmistaken to have excellent experience and realization but no pride or vanity. It is possible that someone who starts to have meditation experiences might think, "Those people are just worldly fools and I am a great practitioner," which is arrogance or pride. He or she might be intoxicated by these experiences and deluded by vanity, thinking, "I must be an arya now. I am really getting close to buddhahood. It is just around the corner." It is important to avoid such reactions to experiences in meditation.

Ninth, it is unmistaken to be independent in solitude and relaxed in the midst of many. This means that you are able to be alone in retreat and take care of yourself, not being in any way disturbed by the lack of company or such things as insufficient clothing and food. You are tough and self-sufficient and you are able to practice in solitude. But at the same time, you are able to be with others when it is appropriate, to be in the midst of an assembly of practitioners without paranoia and without thinking, "I will not be able to get along with them. It will be a real hassle to deal with these people again." You should relax and get along with other people. You have to be able to deal with both situations, and if you can do that, you are a genuine practitioner.

Finally, it is unmistaken to have no attachment to your own benefit, yet be skillful in benefiting others. It is unmistaken if you can be sensitive to the needs of others and apply yourself actively to that which benefits others, but do so without hoping for any kind of gain or return for yourself.

These are the ten things that are unmistaken.

13 The Fourteen Useless Things

Next, there are fourteen things that are totally useless. The first of these is to have obtained a human body but not to remember or think of Dharma. This is as useless as being a poor person who comes to an island covered with many different kinds of jewels, but then leaves the island empty handed, without taking even one jewel.

Second, having entered the door of Dharma through ordination, to then return to worldly life is as useless as a moth being attracted by a candle flame and flying into it.

Third, for someone with no faith to reside in the presence of a great teacher who is a veritable treasury of Dharma is as useless as someone dying of thirst on the border of a lake.

Fourth, to know a great deal about Dharma but not make that knowledge lead to abandoning the four root violations of moral discipline[19] or become an antidote to our ego-clinging is just as useless as placing an ax by the trunk of a tree and not using it to cut down the tree.

Fifth, instructions that are not used as an antidote to kleshas or mental afflictions are as useless as bags of medicine carried around by a sick person and not taken.

Sixth, philosophical terminology in which we have trained our tongue, but which has not been absorbed into our mental continuum, is as useless as the recitations of a parrot.

Seventh, to have taken something that is not given, by means of stealth, overpowering, robbery, deception, or concealment, and then to give it generously to others or use it to make offerings is as useless as to take your sheepskin garment and plunge it into water. This is not so easy to understand because we do not have such things, but a sheepskin garment that is prepared in the traditional way may be dirty, but it is soft. If you try to clean it by putting it in water, when it dries it becomes hard and stiff and totally useless.

Eighth, to harm sentient beings and then offer them to the Three Jewels is as useless as to cut up the flesh of a child and then offer it to the child's mother. This refers to the practice of animal sacrifice that was done in Tibet before the advent of Buddhism. We cannot necessarily call this a Bön practice, because modern Bönpos do not do it. It is something that happened there, and occasionally happens in some places even now. It is considered as useless to offer such things to buddhas and bodhisattvas as it would be to offer the executed body of a son to his mother.

Ninth, to be hypocritically good and patient in order to accomplish our own aims in this life is as useless as the gentle conduct of a cat waiting to pounce on a mouse. Hypocrisy here refers to pretending to be moral when you are not, and patient refers to the patience of waiting for an opportunity to become wealthy or attain some worldly aim. That is like the careful, gentle, and peaceful conduct of a cat that is trying to attract a mouse it wants to kill.

Tenth, to engage in vast acts of virtue in order to become famous or wealthy or honored in this life is like exchanging a wish-fulfilling jewel for a small lump of flour. We might do such things as making and offering statues, or other generally virtuous things, but we might do them just to gain the respect of others, or to attract people so that we might eventually become rich or esteemed within a community. The virtue in itself is like a wishful-filling jewel, but doing such a thing and dedicating it to our own benefit is like exchanging that jewel in order to get a meal. When we dedicate the merit that we accumulate to the benefit of all beings, it becomes inexhaustible like a wish-fulfilling jewel, but not to dedicate it properly is like exchanging that jewel for something that will not last very long.

Eleventh, receiving a great deal of instruction but leaving your own mind untamed is as useless as a physician dying of an incurable disease. The analogy is not very exact or obvious here, but the point is this: If you are very learned in Dharma, and you put a great deal of time and effort in acquiring information, but you have not put any time and effort into practice, it does not help you. It might help somebody else, but it does not help you. That is like the situation of a doctor who is afflicted by a sickness that cannot be cured. A doctor is someone who is very, very learned, but if he or she has a type of sickness that will not respond to medicine, then there is nothing the doctor can do, no matter how skilled he or she is in medicine. This is not saying there is anything wrong with being a doctor, but the point is that study or learning itself cannot actually change everything.

Twelfth, to be learned in instructions but have no experience of practice is like possessing a treasury of wealth to which you have no key.

Thirteenth, to teach Dharma when you have not understood what it means is as useless as for a blind person to lead another blind person.

Fourteenth, to consider the experience that arises from methods of practice as supreme, and not to search for genuine realization of the ultimate nature of the mind, is as useless as to take brass and say it is gold. This refers primarily to the accumulation of merit.[20] If you are satisfied with the accumulation of merit and the experiences or benefits that arise from this, and you do not recognize the nature of all things, then you cannot attain true buddhahood. Thus, when you engage in practices that accumulate merit, it is extremely important to have the intention to accumulate such merit in order to recognize the ultimate nature and attain complete buddhahood. The point here is that method, the accumulation of merit, has to be combined with wisdom, which in this case is the correct realization that you are aiming at. If method and wisdom are not united, your accumulation of merit is no more effective than picking up a yellow stone or a piece of brass and assuming that it is gold.

These are fourteen things that are totally useless. The function of these instructions is to enable you to tell the difference between what is Dharma and what is not Dharma, and to get some idea of how to apply Dharma, how to practice it, what kind of motivation you should have, what happens if that motivation is there, and what happens if that motivation is not there.

14 The Eighteen Hidden Evils of Practitioners

The next category is the eighteen hidden evils of practitioners. Hidden evils here means actions or characteristics that are not in accordance with the aim of a person, in this case a practitioner. For example, if someone is renowned as a scholar but is illiterate, or if someone is renowned as beautiful but has no nose, this is a discordance of name and reality. Thus if someone is renowned as a practitioner but has no practice, that is a discordance of name and reality.

The first of these hidden evils is to reside in solitude and yet only attempt to accomplish greatness in this life. The purpose of residing in solitude is to direct all of your effort to the accomplishment of liberation and omniscience. If instead, while residing in solitude, you direct all your effort to the accomplishment of wealth, renown, service, and comfort, then this is a hidden evil of a practitioner.

Second, to be the leader of a community such as a monastery or some kind of Dharma organization, and yet not take care of it and not make its preservation your aim, but only work to accomplish what seems beneficial to you personally, is a hidden evil of Dharma practitioners.

Third, to be learned in Dharma but not to avoid wrongdoing is a hidden evil of Dharma practitioners. To have the learning that comes from hearing and contemplation, but not to put this into practice by avoiding activities that harm others, is a contradiction of learning and behavior, and therefore is a hidden evil of Dharma practitioners.

Fourth, it is a hidden evil of a practitioner to possess a great deal of instruction but to allow your mental continuum to remain ordinary. This means to have received, understood, and possibly even memorized a great variety of instructions, but for your mind to remain untamed through practice.

Fifth, it is a hidden evil of practitioners to be noble in your physical discipline but to have a mind that is under the power of desire. This means observing a correct moral discipline physically or externally, but not actually taming the mind internally.

Sixth, it is a hidden evil of a practitioner to have a variety of excellent or intense experiences in meditation, but still not to have subdued the mental afflictions.

Seventh, it is a hidden evil of a practitioner to have entered the door of Dharma but not to abandon the attachment and aversion that would afflict an untrained person. This means embarking on the practice of Dharma, yet not relinquishing jealousy, greed, and pettiness.

Eighth, it is a hidden evil of a practitioner to have abandoned mundane activities and entered into the total practice of Dharma, but then bit by bit to return unwittingly to farming, which means to the mundane activities that were abandoned. When people renounce the world, if their renunciation is not complete, what will sometimes happen is that in the beginning they will be pure renunciates and practice Dharma, but then when they are older renunciates they will start to creep back into their old activities.

Ninth, to understand the meaning of Dharma and not to practice it is a hidden evil of a practitioner.

Tenth, to make a great commitment to a period of practice and then not to keep to it is a hidden evil for a Dharma practitioner. For example, to say in the presence of your teacher, "I will remain in retreat for three years," or five years or whatever, and then not be able to do it, is a hidden evil.

Eleventh, to have nothing to do but Dharma and yet not to ameliorate your conduct is a hidden evil of a practitioner. This refers to being in a situation like retreat, where there is absolutely nothing to do except practice, and yet still being concerned with food and clothing and such things.

Twelfth, since, when we practice Dharma, food and clothing will naturally arise through the blessing of the Three Jewels and the power of our practice, it is a hidden evil for a practitioner to worry too much about where these things will come from. This means we should not have thoughts like, "What will I eat tomorrow? What will I wear?"

Thirteenth, to dedicate whatever slight power and merit you have obtained from practice to the magical protection of others from sickness and from *si* is a hidden evil of a practitioner. When a family has a child that dies, there is a concern on the part of the parents that the next child might die also. This is called *si* in Tibetan. People in that situation would ask for some kind of blessing to prevent this from happening. To dedicate your practice to such temporary benefits and to lose sight of the ultimate aim, which is taming your own mental afflictions and developing the ability to tame the mental afflictions of others, and eventually to establish them all in buddhahood, is a hidden evil of a practitioner. This is not saying that it is improper to help people if you have the genuine ability to do so. What is being pointed out as a defect here is doing these things so that people will say you have a lot of magical power and are very worthy of respect—in other words, doing it to acquire a reputation or a following.

Fourteenth, to teach profound instructions in order to obtain food and wealth is a hidden evil of a practitioner. To teach indiscriminately whatever you know, whatever texts you have studied, and whatever practices you can explain, simply to obtain position and wealth and so forth, is a defect. There is a great deal of this nowadays; in fact, this is what we all do.

Fifteenth, it is a hidden evil of practitioners to skillfully and indirectly praise themselves and criticize or revile others. For example, you might say, "I am a completely ordinary teacher. I have no qualities whatsoever, but my lineage is very, very profound and has great blessings that are totally unimpaired. My teachers are so and so, and so and so, and they are very powerful." You would then tell stories about these teachers that make them very interesting and impressive, and continue with, "While I am completely ordinary, the instructions that I have are of great profundity." Then, speaking about other teachers, you would say, "They have extraordinary qualities; they are very learned and accomplished. However, their lineage is a little bit funny. Such and such happened at one time, and then one of their teachers did such and such." In speaking this way, while it appears that we are putting ourselves down and praising others, in fact we are doing the opposite, and this is a hidden evil of practitioners.

Sixteenth, to teach the instructions that you have received to others, but to allow your own mental continuum to remain unsubdued and not in accord with the Dharma, is a hidden evil of practitioners. As was said before, people who receive instructions can become like echoes, so that whatever goes in comes right back out again, but nothing is really happening. In this situation, whatever instructions you receive you pass on to others without practicing them yourself, although you understand what they mean. Someone like that does not develop the qualities for which we attach the name "practitioner."

A practitioner of Dharma is someone who, having received instructions, practices them so that he or she changes. The mental afflictions start to diminish, and compassion and loving-kindness start to increase. That is what it means to be a Dharma person. Someone who just understands things and passes them on is not really a Dharma practitioner, because he or she does not have the qualities to which we can assign that name.

The seventeenth hidden evil of a practitioner is to be unable to remain in solitude, and yet to be unable to get along with others when you are living with them. This is the opposite of one of the ten unmistaken things that were described earlier, when it was said that you should be able to abide in solitary retreat and also, when appropriate, to abide harmoniously in the midst of a community of practitioners. In this case, although you have promised to practice in retreat, when you are in retreat you cannot practice because you are worried that you might not get every little bit of food and clothing you think you need, and you are afraid of being too hot or too cold or something. Then, when you are not in retreat but you are with other people, you are constantly quarreling with them and fighting about insignificant things, so that you cannot get along with anyone. Someone like that is not really a practitioner.

Finally, it is a hidden evil for a practitioner to be unable to withstand happiness or suffering. If you become totally swept away by pleasant circumstances or comfortable conditions so that you lose your mind to that pleasure or that comfort, and if at the same time, when something in your external circumstances makes you slightly uncomfortable or is slightly unpleasant you are immediately cast into a pit of depression, then you are not really a practitioner.

These are the eighteen hidden evils of practitioners.

15 The Twelve Indispensable Things

Next are eleven things[21] without which there is no way to practice genuine Dharma. First, if you do not possess from the very beginning of your practice the stable faith or confidence that comes from a sincere and genuine fear for the sufferings of birth and death, there is no way to practice Dharma. The only thing that can motivate a correct practice of Dharma is such a recognition of the misery of the continuous cycle of birth and death. Only through that recognition can you have a stable confidence in an authentic teacher and his or her instructions, and only with that confidence can you actually come to understand and practice Dharma.

Second, even if you have such a stable confidence, there is still no way to practice Dharma without an authentic guru who can actually direct you on the path that will lead to liberation.

Third, although you have such a teacher, if you do not possess the insight that is the correct understanding of the meaning of Dharma, then there is no way to practice.

Fourth, even if you have such a genuine insight into the meaning of Dharma, if you do not possess the diligence that combines an armor-like, unflagging commitment with genuine courage, there is no way to practice. Armor here means the momentum of having committed yourself so strongly that from the moment you begin to practice, no matter what happens or how long a time goes by, you will never turn away from diligent practice. Courage means being able to get through particular obstacles, adverse conditions, and problems that occur during practice, by turning away from the natural tendency to be so disturbed by these difficulties that you give up.

Fifth, if you have the attitude that whatever practice of the three trainings and gathering of the two accumulations you have done is enough, there is no way to practice genuine Dharma. You can never be content with the amount you have done. As mentioned earlier, the three trainings are personal discipline, meditation, and acquiring correct knowledge or understanding, and the two accumulations are merit and wisdom. It is important never to be content with whatever measure of these trainings and accumulations you have performed.

For example, it is improper if, having finished one hundred thousand mandala offerings, you think, "That's enough merit, I can stop here," or having recited the prescribed number of mantras, you think, "That's enough mantras." Actually your goal is not only to finish a particular practice or accumulate a certain number of mantras, but to obtain the total omniscience of complete buddhahood. To think, "This much is enough, I've done enough," is as foolish as for someone who has decided, "I'm going to walk from here to that city over there," to walk ten steps, or a hundred or even a thousand steps, and then say, "Well, that's enough." Until you get there, until you have finished what you are trying to do and fulfilled your commitment, it is not enough.

Sixth, if you lack the view that is the correct understanding of the nature of all things, then there is no way to practice. In order to achieve the fruition of Dharma practice it is necessary to understand and appreciate the nature of all things. Specifically, we must understand the fact that the wisdom and qualities of the fruition are spontaneously present in the basis, which is our situation right now. It is only because of the presence of such wisdom and qualities that it is possible to remove the habitual and afflictive obscurations that conceal them. Therefore, it is only through this view that we can understand how the fruition can be obtained, and it is only through this view that we can obtain it.

If we do not have this view we will not really understand what defects are to be avoided, what qualities will arise on the path, and how they will arise. We will not know what direction to head in our practice. We will be like people walking blindfolded toward a destination in an unknown direction. No matter how vigorously they walk, they will not have any idea where they are going, so they will never get there. If you have this correct view or understanding, then even if your steps on the path are faltering, few, and slow, you know where you are going. Your eyes are opened and you see your destination, so eventually you will arrive.

Seventh, if you do not possess the meditation that is the ability to place your mind in whatever way and on whatever object you wish, there is no way to practice. The development of tranquility or *shinay* is absolutely vital to the performance of any kind of practice. If you possess some degree of tranquility, you can visualize deities and maintain that visualization, remembering all the details of their appearance. You can recite mantras and direct your attention to each syllable of the visualized mantra. Even if you are performing mundane activities, you will be able to perform them with complete mindfulness and attention, so that whatever you do becomes easy and is performed effectively. Finally, when you come to recognize the ultimate nature, you will be able to rest in it without distraction. As was said by the Great Lord Tsongkhapa, you must have such tranquility that when your mind is at rest it is unmoving like the king of mountains, and when you send it forth it can immediately enter into any act of virtue.

Eighth, without possessing the conduct that brings all of your activities to the path, there is no way to practice Dharma. The general meaning of such conduct is that everything you do is performed with virtuous motivation, virtuous aspiration, virtuous attitude, and virtuous perception. For example, when practitioners are walking up a mountainside they would generate the aspiration, "May all sentient beings ascend the path to complete liberation." When walking down, they would think, "May all buddhas emanate from the dharmakaya in form bodies and bring all sentient beings to liberation." When walking along a road, they would think, "May all sentient beings traverse the correct and proper path without obstacles." When lighting a fire, they would think, "May the fire of wisdom burn the defilements of all sentient beings." All such motivations and practices connected with daily activities can be found in the sutras of the mahayana. The particular meaning with respect to secret mantra is that throughout all activities you should maintain the awareness of yourself as the deity, sound as mantra, and all mental events as the display of wisdom. Through such conduct everything you do becomes meaningful and is brought to the path.

Ninth, unless you receive and actually implement instructions that will enable you to overcome obstacles to practice—not leaving them as mere words—there is no way to do the practice successfully. This refers to instructions that will enable you to transcend impediments and adverse conditions, transcend the seduction of Mara, and recognize and avoid sources of error or corruption in practice. It is especially important that when you receive such instructions you actually put them into practice. Leaving instructions as mere words means to receive instructions from a teacher, memorize them, and repeat them to others, but never make any use of them.

Tenth, there is no way to attain the result or to make practice meaningful without possessing the great confidence that will make you happy at the time of separation of your mind and body. Great confidence comes from making good use of the opportunity to practice. This means that, having obtained a precious human body, you have exerted yourself in hearing, contemplation, and meditation, you have performed benefit directly and indirectly for others, and you have acquired and made use of a pure path. Because you have the confidence that comes from this, should you die at any moment, which might happen, the possibility does not frighten you. This is similar to the feeling of someone who could be driven into exile from his or her country or place of residence at any moment, but knows that the place of exile is somewhere where there are friends, property, and money that can be used to survive. Such a person is not really worried about what will happen.

The best form of this confidence comes from the realization of mahamudra, in which case you know that when you die the path clear light—the realization you have gained through your practice—will mix with the ground clear light, which is the fundamentally present clear light that arises in the awareness of someone who has just died. You know that these will mix in the manner of a child jumping into the lap of its mother, and that when that occurs, you will immediately attain the state of unity, the state of Vajradhara. If you do not have such assurance, then, as the next best form, it is sufficient to have the stable confidence that you have done your utmost in the accumulation of merit and wisdom, and that therefore nothing can go wrong when you die. Generating such confidence that at the time of your death you are safe is the whole point of Dharma.

Finally, there is no way to practice genuine Dharma without having the fruition that is the spontaneous presence within us of the three bodies. The view on which the path of practice is based is the understanding of the nature of all things. While things possess no inherent existence and are therefore said to be empty, there is a lucidity that characterizes our experience, and there is at the same time an unimpededness or unlimited variety to what we experience. That is the way things are, and it is understood through the process of having this nature pointed out at the time of instruction. The recognition of this nature is the starting point and basis for the path, which is familiarization with this nature. This leads to the result, which is the manifestation of the emptiness of all experience as the body of essential qualities or dharmakaya; the manifestation of the inherent lucidity as the body of complete enjoyment or *sambhogakaya;* and the manifestation of the unimpededness as the body of emanation or *nirmanakaya,* which is emanating in an unlimited variety of forms in order to benefit each and every sentient being in whatever way is appropriate for his or her particular situation.

It is necessary to understand that the result of practice is not something that will happen automatically, because the fruition is different from our present state, but neither is it something new, because the nature of the fruition is our nature right now. The fact that it is both new and not new is indicated by the term "spontaneous presence." We can say that the fruition is something new because at this point we do not experience the three bodies of full buddhahood. They are obscured by the adventitious veils that have afflicted us from beginningless time. On the other hand, we cannot really say that the fruition is something new, because what the three bodies really are is present in us and is merely obscured. The fruition consists of the recognition of the three bodies in us and the resultant removal of the obscurations.

These are the eleven things without which there is no way to practice genuine Dharma.

16 The Eleven Marks of a Holy Person

The next list is the eleven marks or indications of a holy person. The first of these is that, no matter whether young or old, male or female, if someone has very little jealousy and very little pride then he or she is a holy or genuine individual.

Second, if someone has very little desire and attachment for pleasures and possessions, and is satisfied with few and simple things, this is an indication that he or she is a holy person.

Third, if someone is devoid of bragging, vanity, and arrogance, this is a sign that he or she is a holy person.

Fourth, if someone is devoid of hypocrisy and behaves exactly the same in public and private, this is an indication that he or she is a holy person. Hypocritical people, for example, are extremely peaceful, subdued, proper, careful, and attentive in the presence of many people, but when they are alone or with a few people they feel they can trust, they are wild, uncontrolled, and undisciplined. Someone who is genuine or holy is the same no matter who is around because these qualities are naturally present in the mind of this person. Hypocritical people will look good when they are around others because they are trying to appear good, but since they do not really possess the qualities of being peaceful and subdued, they are undisciplined when no one is around.

Fifth, when every action in which someone engages is done consciously and with prior consideration and is executed with mindfulness, this is a sign that he or she is a holy person.

Sixth, if someone adheres to the view of the results of actions with the same care with which we would protect our eyes, this is an indication that he or she is holy or genuine. "Adhering to the results of actions" means that since you are confident that wrongdoing leads to suffering, you abstain from all wrongdoing; and since you are confident that virtue or beneficial action leads to happiness, you protect the practice of virtue, causing it to flourish and not be impaired. The degree of adhering to these two modes of conduct, avoidance and cultivation respectively, is compared to the amount of urgency and care with which you would try to protect your eyes if something were about to hit and damage them.

Seventh, if someone makes no distinction between public and private situations in the observance of vows and samaya, this is an indication that he or she is a holy or genuine person. Such a person observes the requirements of whatever discipline has been undertaken for his or her entire life, or for whatever period of time the commitment has been made, and does so no matter who is around to see, no matter whether the conditions that would support such a discipline are present or not, and no matter whether conditions that might lead to the impairment of such a discipline are present or not.

Eighth, to have no partiality with respect to sentient beings and not to differentiate between old friends and new friends is the mark of a holy person. Partiality means thinking these people or these beings are on my side and those people or those beings are on the other side, and therefore having more compassion for some than for others. The Tibetan word *sar drok* means literally "new friends," but it means to pay more attention to new friends. When you first meet people you find them delightful, you smile at them all the time, and you are very attentive and kind to them; but as you continue to know them over a period of time, the smile starts to fade and your attentiveness to their welfare starts to diminish. A holy or genuine person is the same to the people he or she associates with from the time of first being introduced to them until the last time of seeing them.

Ninth, it is a sign that someone is holy or genuine if he or she does not get angry at the wrongdoing of others but is patient with it. Normally, when we hear about or see people doing something that we feel is morally incorrect, we tend to generate the attitude, "Those people are evildoers. They are sinners. They are bad. Oh, they kill animals! They do this; they do that." You have compassion for the beings that have been harmed but not for those who did the harm. A genuine or holy person will have compassion for both, and especially for the people who are doing the evil.

Tenth, it is an unmistaken mark of a holy or genuine person when someone gives all profit and victory to others and takes all loss and disaster upon himself or herself.

Finally, and in summary, if the manner of thinking or the intention with which someone acts, and the manner of acting, are totally different from and superior to the usual mundane way of things, this is a mark of a holy or genuine person.

These are the eleven indications or marks of a holy person. It is not so much the case that by these eleven signs you can determine who else is a holy person, but if you apply them to yourself, you can figure out pretty quickly whether you are holy or not. Sometimes people say, "I do not know if I really want to attain buddhahood or not. Are you a buddha? What is it like?" There is nothing wrong with that question. It makes a great deal of sense, because, aside from the word "buddha" or *sangye*, we do not really know much about it. We do not know what the word means, what the qualities of a buddha are, or what exactly the path that leads to buddhahood consists of.

The function of this type of instruction is to give you some idea of what qualities actually make a buddha so great, what is the nature of the path, and what exactly is happening to someone who is on that path. If you do not know anything about these things—what the result is or what the path is—then of course you will not have any confidence in the path and you will not have any idea whether you want to take that journey. However, if through this kind of instruction you generate a confident understanding of what happens on the path, what the result is, and why a buddha is supreme among beings, then you will naturally develop a great interest in going through that process.

17 The Ten Things of No Benefit

The next list is the ten things of no benefit. What this means is that there is no final or lasting benefit in these things.

The first of these is that no matter how much service you render to this illusory body, it is impermanent and certain to be destroyed, and therefore there is no ultimate benefit in it. No matter how much attention you pay to your appearance, your clothing, your physical situation, or the care of your body, at some time your body and mind will be separated, and all that you have done to your body to preserve it will no longer have any effect and will not determine what experiences you undergo. Obviously this is not to say that eating the proper food and protecting yourself from sickness is of no benefit, because while you are alive you must do these things. The point is that they are not of lasting benefit because eventually your mind and body will be separated.

The second thing that is of no benefit is greed or covetousness for possessions, wealth, and so forth. No matter how attached you are to beautiful, luxurious things or to any kind of possessions, no matter how much you would like to acquire things you see that are possessed by other people, and no matter whether or not you acquire them, when you die you will go naked and with empty hands. Therefore there is no ultimate benefit in these things.

The third thing that is of no benefit is the work you do on your home. No matter how much time you spend on houses, palaces, or castles, and no matter how much work and austerity goes into their construction and maintenance, when you die you will go alone without your house, your castle, or your palace, and even your corpse will be thrown out the door. At the time of your death these things are of no use. This does not refer to temples, because by building or helping to build a place where people practice you help others to generate merit, and therefore accumulate merit for yourself that stays with you.

Fourth, no matter how many things you give to your children and nephews and nieces, and no matter how loving you are to them, at the time of your death they will not be able to protect you or lengthen your life, so there will be no lasting effect to this. What is beneficial at the time of your death is activity that generates virtue and accumulates merit such as offerings and practice and so forth.

Fifth, no matter how much you love your family and friends, and no matter how much you try to please them, when you die you die alone, and at that time there is no benefit to what you have done or the attachment you have had for them.

Sixth, no matter how many children, nephews, nieces, and so forth you have, your relationship with them is impermanent. They will never be content no matter how much you do for them and no matter how much you give them, so that is of no benefit. Eventually the children and younger family members to whom you may have become so attached will leave you. No matter how much you try to do for them, even if you give them your most treasured possessions, it will never be enough for them, and it will never mean as much to them to receive these things as it means to you to give them.

Seventh, no matter how much land you acquire with the aim of holding it for this life, no matter what position you acquire in the community, such as being a government official, no matter how much authority you acquire and how much work you do to acquire it, when you die your connection to that community and to the land that was yours is finished, so it is of no benefit. Saying these things are of no benefit means that attachment to these things is harmful and fixation on these things is harmful. If, on the other hand, you practice and cultivate Dharma, that is of benefit.

Eighth, if you enter into the door of Dharma through receiving ordination, taking empowerments, undertaking practices, and so forth, but do not practice or conduct yourself in accordance with Dharma, then by means of this unfulfilled involvement in Dharma you will throw yourself into the lower realms, so there is no benefit. You might become involved in practice through peer pressure or through knowing people who are involved in it—that is, for social reasons—and, not really earnestly wishing to practice, you might be unable to keep the commitments you have made. Therefore you return to mundane activities and violate the vows and samaya you have assumed, which is a cause of a lower birth.

Ninth, if you have trained your mind in hearing and contemplation and as a result know a great deal, but have not practiced, no matter how much you know about Dharma, at the time of death there will be nothing at your disposal with which to bring the experience of death to the path, and therefore all that you know will be of no benefit. If you do not have the confidence and the ability to contend with the situation of death that comes from having actually practiced, having cultivated the qualities of the path, accumulated merit, and removed obscurations, then at the time of death you will be terrified and agonized and will not be able to contend with it in any way. No matter how much you know, even if you understand what the benefits of the practices are, just knowing the benefits will not help. You must have reaped those benefits.

Finally, no matter how long you remain in the presence of an authentic teacher, if you have no faith in or respect for that teacher, you will not acquire the qualities or receive the blessings of the teacher, and therefore it is of no benefit.

These are the ten things that are of no lasting benefit.

QUESTIONS AND ANSWERS

Q: In the fourteen things that are totally useless, the fourth was to know a lot about the Dharma if such knowledge does not lead to abandoning the four root violations of moral conduct. What are the four root violations of moral conduct?

A: The text says that to know a great deal of Dharma and yet for it not to be a remedy for the false imputation of an inherently existent self and for it not to lead to the abandonment of the four roots is useless. The four roots are the four actions that lead to the complete eradication of any of the three forms of individual liberation ordination. They are: to kill, to take what is not given, to engage in improper sexual conduct, and to pretend to have superhuman powers—meaning to lie about spiritual attainments.

There are, as you may know, three types of individual liberation ordination: that of a *genyen* or lay disciple, a *getsul* or novice, and a *gelong* or fully ordained monk or nun. In the case of a *genyen*, the third root, improper sexual conduct, means adultery or *logyem*. In the case of a *tsang chö genyen* or celibate lay disciple, a *getsul*, or a *gelong*, it means any sexual activity whatsoever. Those are the four roots.

In regard to Dharma becoming a remedy for ego-clinging, this means that the practice of Dharma should serve to help us come to the recognition that there is no inherently existent self, and at the same time, to help us abandon or work through the habit of imputing the existence of such a self. If Dharma practice does not do these two things—serve as an antidote to ego-clinging and help us avoid these four types of actions—then it is said to be useless.

Q: Did you say under the things to be known, in number six, that the longer karma takes to ripen the more weight it has?

A: Not necessarily, because there are two situations that come into this. One is that if a tremendously powerful negative action is performed, it is likely to mature very quickly, possibly in this same life or in the life immediately after; so in that case, it is not true that the sooner it matures the less heavy the ripening will be. The other is when a practitioner who has cultivated compassion gets ill or experiences some relatively minor ripening of previous karma and makes the aspiration, "May all my other negative karma be experienced right now, in the context of this situation, and may all the negative karma of all sentient beings be experienced by me right now." On the basis of that unpleasant experience, karma is being purified, which prevents it from being experienced in the future. But this is not so much because the experience itself is a minor result of an action that itself might yield something greater, but because on the basis of that action, the practitioner is making an aspiration and generating an attitude that in itself purifies karma.

Q: In relation to that, if we wish that all our bad karmic results come to fruition, say, right now or in this lifetime, because we want them out of the way, does that mean we are asking for it? We could get very, very sick.

A: If you make the aspiration, "May all the negative karma that I would otherwise have to experience in the future be experienced right now," it will neither increase nor decrease the actual circumstances of suffering that you have to undergo. If you are suffering from a specific sickness, and make that aspiration, it will not remove the physical sickness, and it will not cause a lot of other disasters to start happening. What it will do is strengthen your mind in the ability to accept suffering, so in that sense it will remove your real suffering, your real misery. Normally, the ideas of suffering, misery, sickness, and death are very depressing and generate a great deal of aversion. If you were to go to someone and say, "You are going to get sick and you are going to die," the person would get angry and would not be happy, so there is some effort involved in accepting sickness and suffering.

The point at which a lot of adverse conditions can arise for practitioners is when they attain the first bodhisattva level, at which point they become "noble ones" or aryas. In the lifetime in which they attain the first bodhisattva level they will undergo a lot of adverse conditions, such as sicknesses and obstacles and so forth. The reason is that when such people die, from the succeeding life onwards, they are not really in samsara in the fullest sense, because they have attained so much that they will not experience manifest suffering any more. So in order to transcend it, they have to go through it all very fast, and this happens automatically. They experience a lot of, from their point of view, minor causes of suffering and purify all the remaining karma.

Q: From the Buddha's point of view there is no past, present, and future. Therefore, ultimately there is no past, so is it possible to change the past? Are all the events happening around us attributable to karma? What is the place for free will?

A: The state of buddhahood is not a composite thing. It is not made up of different things coming together, and therefore it is not impermanent and cannot be divided. There is no distinction of past, present, and future within the state of buddhahood itself, because the three times are a process of change, and only apply to impermanent, changeable things. Ultimately, the idea of the three times, of there being an inherently existent past, present, and future, is deceptive, since these are not inherently existent but only relative. The concepts past, present, and future have no ultimate validity; they have only conventional validity.

It is definitely true that our basic situation—how we experience the world, the type of senses and bodies we have, and so forth—results from our previous actions, from our previous karma. In that sense, we cannot change our basic situation. For example, as human beings we experience the world in a certain way. We experience what we call fire as fire, we experience water as water, and so forth. We cannot change that within the context of this life. We cannot change fire to water. Fire will always burn us if we put our hands in it, and so forth. However, you can make moral choices, and the moral choices you make, such as abstaining from that which is harmful and practicing that which is virtuous, do affect your future. You always have choice, and therefore some degree of free will, within the limits of your established perceptions. Those limitations are imposed upon you by your previous karma. However, you can change your future perception and therefore your future limitations by your actions in the present.

Q: Concerning the list of ten things of no final benefit, you said that there is no final benefit in building a house, but you made an exception for building monasteries, in that there is merit to building monasteries. I was wondering whether the merit that one achieves in building monasteries continues after death, or whether it is similar to the rest of the list of ten and also ends upon death.

A: It benefits you in this life; we have a nice place to meet! Actually, it depends upon the intention of the individual involved in the work. If, in building a monastery, your intention is to establish a comfortable and pleasant situation for yourself, then your intention is to benefit yourself, and you will not accumulate any merit that will last beyond this life. But if your intention is to create a place where images of the Buddha, texts, and so forth can be established as objects of people's veneration and bases for their instruction, so that they can accumulate merit, and especially if you build it with the intention that it be a place where as many people as possible can be involved in hearing, contemplation, and meditation on the Dharma, then you have a pure intention. With that pure intention and the pure application of that intention to the building of the monastery, a great deal of merit can be accumulated; and this results in the purification of previous wrongdoing and in the experience of the result of merit, which will most often be in a future life. However, it can happen that merit accumulated in this life is of such intensity that it fully matures in this life.

Q: If intention is the key, could one not build a house or a boat or even a baseball park with the intention of helping others, and would that not have a similar effect?

A: If you build your house, thinking, "I am building this house so that I have a place where I can practice, and I will make use of the house to help other people come in contact with the Dharma," and that is really your intention, then of course you can accumulate merit that will last. What is spoken of in the text is building houses and residences and so forth out of attachment, aversion, and bewilderment, which is different. As far as boats are concerned, of course, if you are building a boat and your intention is that it be of help to sentient beings, then you accumulate merit. As far as ball parks are concerned, if you build a ball park and your whole intention is to cause happiness and pleasure to others, then you will accumulate some merit. However, in that example, the place you build is basically where people can go to become more distracted, so you would not accumulate the same merit that you would in creating an environment where people can engage in the pure practice of Dharma, such as a monastery.

Q: In regard to the accumulation of merit, sometimes we receive newsletters from the monastery or from Buddhist groups saying that if you donate money or do a certain action, you will accumulate much merit. Should we have the attitude, "Oh good, then I will have more that I can dedicate?" It has often bothered me to look at something that seems to be a good idea and then to read at the bottom, "Plus you are going to get lots of merit." That sort of spoils it, because it reinforces the idea of accumulation for self.

A: Well, I cannot say that to make offerings to a monastery in order to accumulate merit is an impure motivation. We have to be realistic, and as beginners, not everyone has the complete motivation of bodhicitta. No matter how elevated or pure a practitioner you are, you still do benefit from your daily practice, the recitations and so forth that tame your mind. Especially in a period of training, the first person to be benefited really is yourself. When people get sick, they make offerings and request blessings and so forth to alleviate the sickness, and there is nothing wrong or ignoble about that. It is hard to completely abandon any concern for our own benefit at the beginning.

From the point of view of the cultivation of bodhicitta, the most perfect motivation is to do everything with the intention of only benefiting others, and not to care at all about our own benefit. That is the best possible intention, but beginners cannot always generate it. It depends upon how far they have gone in the cultivation of bodhicitta. If such an appeal for money for building a monastery or something like that is sent out, then people who have bodhicitta will be inspired by the thought of making offerings to the monastery. They will make those offerings, if they can, because they have bodhicitta, and they will naturally dedicate the merit to all sentient beings, so promising them merit does not prevent them from doing that. Many people that the appeal will reach are not particularly intense practitioners. No matter what the appeal says, it will not instantly transform the motivation of such people to bodhicitta, but the promise of merit might appeal to them, so I cannot say that there is anything wrong with that. Of course, trying to accumulate merit without dedicating it is not the final or ultimate motivation.

Q: Do you get more merit by practicing with other people than alone?

A: Yes, definitely. You accumulate more merit by practicing with other people, because when many people practice together, each person accumulates the benefit of one person multiplied by the number of people that are there. For example, if ten people practice together, each experiences ten times the amount of benefit he or she would experience through practicing alone. It is said that this is the same with negative actions as well. If one group makes war on another group, and one person within one group kills one person within the other group, each person in the killing group accumulates the karma of that killing. So if many kill many, then each person accumulates a lot. This is taught in the *chö ngön pa*, the *abhidharma.*

Q: My question relates to the first two of the ten deviations, relating to faith and intelligence. When I was young, I found it very easy and natural to have faith in things and in myself; but after I grew older, I did not have much faith in things such as medicine, the government, or myself for that matter. Seeing the Dharma, listening to its teachings, and practicing it, I found that it made sense to me as an intellectual. I want to know if there is a difference between having trust in the Dharma and having faith in the Dharma, and also I want to know how we can arouse faith in ourselves toward the path, toward the Dharma, toward the teacher, and toward this text.

A: It is a good sign that you had a naive faith when you were a child, because it indicates a positive disposition. But it is also a very good sign that as you matured, with your growing insight, you examined things and you lost that naïveté. You should not be in any way alarmed by the loss of innocence.

Then, as far as the difference between faith and trust is concerned, the function of intelligence from a Dharmic point of view is to be able to see defects and qualities clearly, and to be able to distinguish between what is to be accepted and what is to be rejected. The way to make use of intelligence is to examine every aspect of the Dharma step by step, and then you can trust what you have proven to yourself to be valid through that examination. This is different from the kind of naive faith that you experienced when you were a child, because this trust is based on, and only proceeds as far as, what you have determined to be valid through applying your intelligence.

Basically, the reason this is possible, and why there is validity to the application of a developed insight or intelligence, is that the mind of any one of us has in its nature the capacity or inherent potential to generate all positive qualities and anything good that is imaginable. The difference between our minds at different times, and the difference between the minds of different people, depends upon the situation, and what is contained in their minds. In our minds we have both positive qualities, such as love and compassion, and negative ones, such as mental afflictions and ignorance. It is important to make use of the inherent intelligence of your mind to examine carefully everything that you have to deal with, the way you examine substances to determine whether they are medicine or poison. Having examined such substances, you accept the medicine and avoid the poison. When coming into contact with Dharma, you examine it in detail and with great care, and then, just as you would determine a medicine to be useful and not poisonous, bit by bit you will come to trust those aspects of Dharma that you have proven to yourself to be valid. This not only gives you confidence in the Dharma, it also exercises and develops the intelligence with which you can analyze Dharma.

Having done that, you can practice, and the practice is based upon this faith or trust you develop in the Dharma. This trust is based upon intelligence and application, and it is different from the innocent or naive trust of a child, which is based on an absence of experience. It is not based on any examination and there is no certainty in the depth of it. Attempting to maintain a naive faith without examination will lead to failure, because the trust of a child will change; whereas trust that is developed on the basis of your own validation of Dharma through your own reasoning will not change, because it has been proven. Thus, the way to deal with your situation is simply to listen to and contemplate the Dharma, and to engage in the process of study and analysis.

Q: One of the deviations you mentioned yesterday was that if you do not immediately put into practice your understanding of Dharma, your desire to use it becomes less and less and your inspiration becomes jaded or tired. If that happens, how does one rekindle the inspiration? More specifically, when I first took refuge, the four thoughts—the precious human birth, impermanence, karma, and samsara—were very inspiring and very strong motivations for me, but now, somehow they do not give me the same inspiration.

A: The solution to becoming jaded about Dharma is to examine yourself honestly. The most important thing is to look at your own mind and examine your own situation, because if you see that you are becoming callous or insensitive to Dharma, then the recognition of that will lead to removing the defect. For example, if you are walking somewhere and all of a sudden you see in front of you an abyss or a raging fire into which you might fall, just seeing it will make you step back and avoid it.

Q: My wife and other people that I have encountered recently have very severe reservations about participating in ritual and puja. They may be willing to listen to teachings, they may be willing to meditate, but they are not interested in puja or ritual. How should I deal with this situation, and what is the purpose of ritual and puja in Buddhism?

A: It is very good when someone, for example your wife, likes to hear teachings and likes to meditate. The only reason that someone who likes those things does not like ritual and practices that make use of different kinds of elements is that they do not see any point to it. They do not understand what the benefits of such things are, and so, of course, they have no respect for them, and just think, "What use is all that ritual?"

The reason for these practices is that whatever we do in the world, whatever wrongdoing and virtue we perform, we do with the body, speech, and mind. We do things, we say things, and we think things. Especially, we have been engaging in physical wrongdoing, verbal wrongdoing, and mental wrongdoing over a period of time that has no beginning. To reverse that habitual tendency and remove the obscuration of those actions, it is necessary to cultivate virtue with the same three faculties: with body, with speech, and with mind. For example, we cultivate virtue with body by performing circumambulation and prostrations, with speech by the recitation of mantras and supplications, and with mind by the cultivation of loving-kindness, compassion, and so forth.

If you want to get somewhere you actually have to walk, which involves using your legs; you cannot just sit there and imagine it. Likewise, in practice you have to make use of every aspect of yourself. Nevertheless, even though someone may not appreciate the value of ritual and practices that make use of physical and verbal elements, it is still very good that they are open to the ideas and concepts of Dharma and the practice of meditation.

Q: How do you avoid falling into the formless realm, and what is it? Is it a hell realm? It sounds terrifying, actually.

A: We are not in the slightest danger of being reborn in the formless realm, because the only possible cause for rebirth in the formless realm is to have absolutely perfect tranquility, such that you see all worldly pleasures as your enemies and have complete and absolute disgust for everything, and you live in total solitude, in a state of complete and utter absorption without any kind of conceptuality whatsoever.

The formless realm is not really a place or a specific thing; it is an experience that happens. When someone like that dies, the person undergoes an experience, and if you can describe it as happening in a place, the person remains where he or she dies. It is an experience with absolutely no pleasure and absolutely no suffering, and because there is no pleasure and no suffering, it is an experience of total tranquility, and it lasts for an extremely long time—many, many *kalpas*. There are two problems with it. One is that when the merit or the momentum of the previous meditation that generated that experience is finally exhausted, even though it does take a very long time, the person is reborn again in some other form of life where there is suffering. The second problem is that if it happens accidentally to extremely advanced practitioners who slip into that kind of absorption, it is a tremendous obstacle to the practice of Dharma, because it delays them for so long.

Q: Concerning the list in which you differentiated between authentic teachers and charlatans of various sorts, I was wondering what the point of that teaching was, and how you would reconcile that with two things you said earlier. The first is that sometimes the people who are the worst to us can be our best teachers because they show us either obstacles to our minds or different aspects of ourselves; and the second is the tantric view of seeing all situations and all people as our own guru.

A: The advice to distinguish carefully between authentic teachers and charlatans is for those at the beginning of the path, at the point where they have to choose a teacher. At the beginning of the path you do not know anything, and you definitely need the instruction and advice of someone authentic. Also, at the beginning of the path you do not have the power to take enemies as teachers, to see the aggression of others as an exhortation to realization, and so forth. Having received instruction from a genuine teacher, when you practice his or her instructions, you then need to be able to bring to the path whatever adverse conditions occur; so the second piece of advice, to regard all enemies and obstructers as teachers, is given to guide the perception and conduct of individuals engaged in intense practice who have to contend with adverse conditions. Thus, this advice applies at a different time.

Also in the teachings of secret mantra it is said that the view of an advanced practitioner should be that of seeing everything as the mandala of the guru, or boundless purity and equality. This refers to a level of practice in which, having recognized the nature of your mind as wisdom, you recognize everything you experience as the display of the lucidity of that wisdom. This is something that really only applies and happens to quite advanced practitioners.

Q: As beginning practitioners, it is difficult to know our own intentions, so how are we to figure out the intentions of others, especially charlatans or advanced teachers who are way beyond us?

A: When I say "beginner" here, I do not mean someone who has never seen a text of Dharma or has never heard of Dharma. I mean someone who has generated a certainty about the validity and value of Dharma, someone who, through the influence of friends, through reading books, or some such means or combination of means, has come to recognize the qualities of Dharma, what Dharma means, and what the benefits of it are.

A person in that position has some ability to make decisions about his or her own education. The next step is to find a teacher, and when you first meet a teacher it is important to examine the teacher, to listen to what he or she says and to see if it makes sense and is helpful, to watch how the teacher acts and see if it seems to be appropriate.

It was said by the eminent teacher Paltrul Rinpoche, "In the beginning be skillful in examining the lama." At the beginning, before you enter into a relationship with a teacher, you have to examine to see if the teacher is genuine or not. However, once you have taken on someone as a teacher, once you have received Dharma instructions and empowerment from that teacher, and have taken samaya vows with respect to that teacher, then you have to continue to rely upon him or her. If you examine your teacher and see a defect at that point, you run into the danger of violating your samaya. Paltrul Rinpoche also said, "In the middle be skillful in relying on the lama."

Q: If you do find a teacher to be a charlatan, and you have a samaya vow with that teacher, then since this is not a legitimate teacher, would that mean the samaya vow is not legitimate to begin with?

A: First of all the bestowal of authentic empowerment is not something easy. In order to bestow empowerment you must have received not only the empowerment and the transmissions, but also the complete instructions for the meditation and practices connected with the empowerment, and as well, the complete instructions for giving the empowerment and related matters. Then you must have practiced all of these. The practice consists of three types of extensive accumulations of mantra, which are called "the three measures of approach to realization." These are measuring the approach by number—how many mantras; measuring the approach by time—how long spent in retreat; and measuring the approach by signs or indication of realization.

Of these three the main one for someone who is going to give empowerment is signs or indication. In order to give empowerment one has to have actually experienced the specific signs connected with the realization of the specific deity and practice. Then, having gone through this process, one is allowed to perform empowerment, consecration, the fire offering, and so forth, provided that in addition one receives the specific instructions and authorization to do so from the lineage holder who possesses that particular teaching. Anyone who has gone through this entire process is not a charlatan.

On the other hand, if someone gives empowerments because he or she is clever and knows how to read the text and can figure out what to do, whether or not the person actually has the empowerment or has the authorization of the lineage, and if you take an empowerment in that situation, then I cannot say that you actually have samaya vows. For example, if I hand you an empty cup and I say, "Have some tea," and you go through the motions of drinking, there is nothing in the cup, so I cannot say that you have had any tea. However, even in such a situation, because the motions have been gone through and the words have been said, and because you were undertaking the process of empowerment, whatever the other person was doing, you have made a connection at least in form, so I cannot say that you do not have samaya vows. It is a very difficult process and I cannot say one way or the other.

However, practically speaking, when people have entered into a relationship with a teacher and subsequently decide that their teacher is a charlatan, usually it seems to be the projection of their own impure motivation. The problem is that in the section of the text that deals with things that are easy to mistake for each other, it really means *for each other*. The mistake could go either way. Just as it is possible to mistakenly see a charlatan as a siddha, it is equally possible to mistakenly see a siddha as a charlatan, so one has to watch out for both errors.

Q: If someone has golden light above his head, does that mean he will certainly be reborn in the pure land?

A: I do not know. It is possible, I suppose, that having golden light shining above your head could be a sign of having received the blessings of the compassion of the buddhas and bodhisattvas, because it is possible for different kinds of experiences or indications to occur as a result of receiving these blessings. But I cannot say and I have not seen it written anywhere that having golden light shining above your head is a certain indication of rebirth in Sukhavati, the pure land.

However, it sounds like something positive, because sometimes things like this do happen. The previous incarnation of Dzongsar Khyentse Rinpoche passed away in 1959 in Sikkim, and the day he passed away, all the people in the area saw the entire country to be golden in color. No one except the people in his house knew he was passing away that particular day. People found out afterwards that at the time when they experienced the golden color, Dzongsar Khyentse Rinpoche was passing into peace.

18 The Ten Ways of Accomplishing Your Own Disaster

Next are the ten situations of accomplishing your own disaster. The first of these is when a single Dharma practitioner marries and then finds that there is no opportunity to practice because of the responsibilities that go with that, such as raising children and so forth. Such a living situation, rather than being supportive to practice, becomes an obstacle to Dharma practice and a source of rebirth in the lower realms. This is similar to a foolish person eating strong poison because he or she likes the color or smell of it.

The second situation of accomplishing your own disaster is when someone has attained a human existence with the opportunity to practice Dharma, and then does not practice but engages in wrongdoing. This is like an insane person jumping off a cliff. Insanity here is a metaphor for the situation of not practicing Dharma when you have the opportunity to do so, and jumping off a cliff is a metaphor for engaging in wrongdoing.

The third way of accomplishing your own disaster is to violate your vows and samaya, and then on top of that become a charlatan who deceives others and pretends to be a genuine teacher. This is like eating poisoned food, which might temporarily alleviate hunger, but will also cause death. Likewise, you may deceive others, thinking that in the short run this will be of some help, but in the long run, you will only accomplish your own disaster.

The fourth situation is for someone of little intelligence to become the director of a monastic or secular community. This is like forcing a very old person who can hardly move to guard cattle. This situation refers to someone without the ability to direct an organization or community in a beneficial and skillful way.

The fifth way of accomplishing your own disaster is not to be diligent in the accomplishment of benefit for others through an excellent motivation, but instead to exert yourself in the accomplishment of your own aims through the motivation of the eight things of the world—desire for praise and acquisition and so forth. This is like a blind person wandering around in the wilderness or in a vast desert. By not engaging in that which benefits others with a good motivation, you have no opportunity to accumulate merit. On top of that, by engaging in that which would seem to benefit yourself with acquisition, gain, praise, and so forth as your motivation, you will not accomplish any good for yourself in this life, and you will accumulate the cause for tremendous suffering in future lives. In a similar way, a blind person who is thrust into the middle of a desert or a wilderness has no way to find his or her destination.

Sixth, to undertake a great and difficult endeavor that you have no way of accomplishing, and to commit yourself to this, is accomplishing your own disaster. It is like a very weak person trying to carry an extremely heavy burden.

Seventh, to disregard through arrogance the instructions or advice of an authentic teacher and the recorded instructions and advice of the Buddha is accomplishing your own disaster. This is like a powerful leader not listening to wise counselors. As an illustration of this, a long time ago there was a particular monastery in eastern Tibet, in Kham. In the same region as the monastery there was a powerful nobleman who was not particularly associated with the monastery in any way. He was having a quarrel with the imperial Chinese government, and they were preparing to invade his territory. The monastery was quite powerful in the region, so this lord appealed to its leaders and said, "Will you support me in my struggle with the imperial government?" The monastic council discussed this request, and most members said, "No, we should not get involved in this dispute. It is not really our business." But one very powerful and outspoken member of the monastic council said, "We should help this nobleman because then if he wins he will be in our debt. We will be able to spread our influence into his territory and he will be under us." He was so strong in his argument that they were swayed by him and supported the nobleman. As it happened, the Chinese won, and they destroyed not only the nobleman's territory but the monastery as well, because the monastery had supported him. That is an illustration from long ago of this type of situation.

The eighth way of accomplishing your own disaster is if, having studied and contemplated the Dharma, you do not practice it but instead procrastinate and wander among the habitations of people. This is like a wild animal that does not stay in the mountains where it is safe, but wanders into the regions of humans and is therefore killed.

Ninth, having received an introduction to or pointing out of natural wisdom from your teacher, not to foster this through practice, but to be diverted by the elaboration of distraction, is accomplishing your own disaster. This is like being a bird with a broken wing. Just as a bird with a broken wing still has wings, you still have received the introduction, the pointing out, but the power of it has been broken by your involvement in distraction.

Tenth, carelessly consuming the possessions and wealth of your guru and the Three Jewels will accomplish your own disaster. This is like a small child who sees a burning ember in the fire and, attracted by the red color, grabs it and puts it in his or her mouth. This means to take things that are offered to support teachers and the monastic community, and consume them for the sake of enjoyment and luxury.

Those are ten situations of accomplishing your own disaster.

19 The Ten Things That Are Great Kindnesses to Yourself

Then come ten situations of great kindness to yourself. First, to abandon attachment and aversion for the things of this world and to practice genuine and pure Dharma is a great kindness to yourself, because in doing so you will bring about your own liberation, which is the ultimate and final accomplishment of your own benefit.

Second, to remain single and to abandon friends and family, relying instead upon holy or genuine individuals, is a great kindness to yourself.

Third, to abandon distraction and engage instead in hearing, contemplating, and meditating is a great kindness to yourself. Even when you are attending upon or in the presence of an authentic teacher, it is possible that you might still devote yourself to subduing enemies and pleasing your friends. To abandon all these distractions and meaningless activities and to put the instructions into actual practice through hearing, contemplation, and meditation is a great kindness to yourself.

Fourth, to abandon too much familiarity with people through living with them and being subjected to their whims, and instead to abide alone in solitude is a great kindness to yourself.

Fifth, abiding in solitude will not work if you are still attached to all the things that you are without. Thus, when abiding in solitude, to cut through attachment to pleasures and desirable things and to abide in a stable state of nonattachment is a great kindness to yourself.

Sixth, in that situation you have to be satisfied with enough clothing so that you do not freeze and enough food so that you do not starve. To be satisfied with what is barely sufficient and to have no interest in or desire for fine things is a great kindness to yourself.

Seventh, by not surrendering your independence and the choice of your actions of body, speech, and mind to another, to allow your practice to be stable and unimpeded is a great kindness to yourself. This does not mean that you cannot cooperate with other people or give and receive benefit from them; it means that in the context of practice, when you have what you need, you should not surrender your independence to anyone else.

Eighth, to pay no attention to the ephemeral pleasures of this life but earnestly to accomplish the awakening that is permanent happiness is a great kindness to yourself.

Ninth, in the context of practice, to abandon all fixation on the apparent solidity of experienced things and to cultivate the realization of emptiness is a great kindness to yourself.

Tenth, when abiding in solitude, not to allow your body, speech, and mind to slip into ordinariness but to exert yourself in the unified accomplishment of the two accumulations is a great kindness to yourself.

These are the ten things that are of great kindness to yourself.

20 The Ten Perfect Things

Next come the ten things that are perfect. First, to have trust in the results of actions is the perfect view for a beginner. This means to recognize that wrongdoing will lead to suffering and that virtue will lead to happiness.

Second, recognizing that all inner and outer things are the unity of awareness and emptiness and the unity of appearance and emptiness is the perfect view for an intermediate practitioner. This refers to the view connected with the practice of the bodhisattvayana.

Third, to realize that that which is viewed, the viewer, and the realization itself are indivisible or undifferentiated is the perfect view for an advanced practitioner or someone of the highest capabilities. This refers principally to the vajrayana level, but such a view can also be present in the practice of mahayana, especially during the actual meditation sessions.

Fourth, to abide with a mind that is one-pointedly directed to the object of meditation, that is, to abide in a consummate state of tranquility, is the perfect meditation for a beginner.

Fifth, in the same way, to abide in the *samadhi* (meditative absorption) that is the recognition of the four unities is the perfect meditation for an intermediate practitioner. The four unities are the unity of appearance and emptiness, of sound and emptiness, of bliss and emptiness, and of awareness and emptiness.

Sixth, to abide in the nonconceptual state in which that on which one meditates, the meditator, and the practice are recognized to be indivisible is the perfect meditation of someone of the highest faculties or the most advanced practitioner. This is the supreme practice of both sutrayana and tantrayana, and it is known as not conceptualizing the three aspects of any situation.

Seventh, to guard your adherence to the principle of cause and result of actions as carefully as you guard your eyes is the perfect conduct for a beginner.

Eighth, to conduct yourself with the recognition that all things that you experience are like a dream or a magical illusion, a recognition that comes out of meditation practice, is the perfect conduct for someone of intermediate faculties or at an intermediate level, which is someone practicing the bodhisattva path.

Ninth, engaging in no conduct whatsoever is the perfect conduct of an advanced practitioner or someone of superior faculties. This means having no concept of what is conduct, what is not conduct, and so forth.

There are two ways of understanding these three sets of three. Sometimes, people understand them as meaning that first you practice what is appropriate for a beginner; then, when you become an intermediate practitioner, you abandon that and change to the intermediate practitioner's way of doing things; and when you become an advanced practitioner, you abandon that also. This is practicing the three exclusively and sequentially.

The other way of understanding it is that as a beginner, you practice what is appropriate for a beginner; then as you become more advanced, you continue practicing that but add to it what is suitable for an intermediate practitioner; and when you become an advanced practitioner, you continue those two practices and add to them the insight of an advanced practitioner. The second way of viewing these is the correct one; they are practiced sequentially but not exclusively. In other words, do not throw away the lower levels when you proceed to the higher ones.

The tenth perfect thing is the progressive diminishing and pacification of all fixation on an inherently existent self, and of all mental affliction. This is the perfect, correct, and genuine sign of successful practice for someone of any of the three faculties—lesser, intermediate, or greater, or any of the three levels.

These are the ten perfect things.

21 The Ten Bewilderments of Practitioners

Next come the ten bewilderments of practitioners. First, not to rely on an excellent teacher who practices Dharma properly but to rely upon a cleverly spoken charlatan is a case of extreme bewilderment.

Second, not to search for the precious instructions of the oral lineage of siddhas but to exert yourself in the study of logic and reasoning is extremely bewildered.

Third, not to be content with whatever appearances arise in the present, but to make extensive preparations for the future based on the assumption that things will remain the same, is extremely bewildered.

Fourth, not to think about Dharma while living alone, but to teach it in the midst of others, is extremely bewildered.

Fifth, not to use your excess wealth and possessions for offerings and generosity to others, but to accumulate wealth and possessions stealthily, is extremely bewildered. This means that, although you have a lot of money, you do not share any of it with other people who may not have enough food or other things, nor do you make offerings with it. When it is time to make offerings or perform any act of generosity, you say, "I don't have anything. I can't give anything. I'm sorry, I wish I could," and meanwhile you are accumulating a pile of money.

Sixth, not to guard whatever vows and samaya you have undertaken, but to let your body, speech, and mind run wild, is extremely bewildered. This means, for example, that you have committed yourself to the practice of Dharma and to a certain discipline of conduct, but as soon as a movie comes out, you have to go and see it; if something exciting happens in town, you have to be part of it; if there is boxing on television, you have to watch it; or if there is a new place to go dancing, you have to go there the first night it opens.

Seventh, not to devote your time and energy to gradual familiarization with the meaning that is to be realized through practice, but to waste your life in meaningless social or political activities, is extremely bewildered.

Eighth, not to tame your own mind or transcend the confusion that arises in your own experience, but rashly attempting to tame the minds of others, is extremely bewildered. If you do not first tame your own mind, then attempting to tame the minds of others or alleviate the bewilderment of others will not work, because you will still be so confused that you will not know how to do it, and you will probably only generate mental affliction. For example, when someone walks between two people who are fighting and tries to separate them and pacify the situation, often the person who is intervening gets angry, and then there are three people fighting instead of two.

Ninth, not to foster the progressive development of qualities that arise through your experience of practice, such as faith, compassion, and so forth, but instead to foster the development of greatness in this life, such as a high position in a community or monastery, fame, wealth and so forth, is extremely bewildered.

Finally, at this time, when the necessary causes and conditions for the opportunity to practice Dharma are present, not to be diligent but to delight in laziness and indolence is extremely bewildered.

These are the ten types of bewilderment.

22 The Ten Necessary Things

Next come ten things that are necessary. First, in the beginning, you need to have the genuine and sincere faith that is based upon fear of the sufferings of samsara, such as birth, death, and so forth, like the attitude of a deer that has escaped from the pit prepared for it by hunters.

Second, in the middle stage, while practicing, you have to have the type of diligence that will leave you without guilt or fear at the time of death, like the attitude of a farmer at harvest time.

Third, in the end, you need to have a happy mind that cannot die, like the attitude of someone who has just accomplished something tremendous.

Fourth, in the beginning, you have to have a sense of urgency, like someone who has just been shot by an arrow. If you have been shot by an arrow, you do not think, "Perhaps before I pull this arrow out, I'll have a cup of tea," or anything like that.

Fifth, in the middle stage, you have to have a meditation that is as undistracted as the sorrow of a mother whose only child has just died. Such a mother thinks only of her sorrow night and day.

Sixth, in the end, you have to have a recognition that there is nothing to do, like cattle freed from their confines by rustlers. When people own cattle, of course, they are always milking them and doing this, that, and the other thing to them, and the cattle have a lot of work and hassles. When rustlers come along and break down the barrier confining the cattle, and the cattle can just wander around, they have a sense of freedom and release.

Seventh, in the beginning, you have to have a certainty towards Dharma like that of a very hungry person who encounters excellent food.

Eighth, in the middle stage, you have to have a certainty about your own mind like that of the wrestler when he found the jewel. This refers to a fable, a story that is allegorical: Once there was a wrestler whose family had given him a diamond, which he always wore on his forehead. He had just won a wrestling match in which he and the other wrestler had both been quite beaten up and had wounds and swellings all over their faces and heads. He was not the least bit disturbed about his wounds, but he was disturbed because he could not find his jewel, and he thought he had lost it. He went all over trying to find it, looking around the wrestling pit, but he could not find it anywhere. Then he went to a physician, who said, "You have a lot of wounds. I had better start fixing them up."

The wrestler said, "I don't care about that! What I care about is that I've lost my family diamond." But the physician insisted on looking at the wounds, and noticed especially one big swollen wound right on his forehead. The doctor asked, "Now how did you lose that diamond?" And the wrestler said, "Well, I was butting him with my head and struggling with him."

The doctor looked inside the swelling and found that the diamond had become stuck under the skin. He told the wrestler, "Here is your diamond." The wrestler was overjoyed when he found that he had not lost the diamond after all. His looking outside for it had been meaningless, because the diamond had not gone out, it had gone in and been hidden. This point refers to having the certainty that the qualities to be realized are found inside the mind and are not to be searched for outside of it.

This type of brief reference to fables is quite common in Gampopa's writings, and also in some of the songs that Milarepa sang to Gampopa, which can be found in *The Rain of Wisdom*.[22]

Ninth, at the end, you have to generate a certainty about nonduality that is like exposing the deception of an impostor. It is necessary to cut through totally the false imputation of the duality of the experiencer and the experience, by determining that all experiences are unestablished as having a nature other than the experience itself.

Tenth, it is necessary to have a final resolution of the meaning of suchness that is like a raven flying free from a cage or ship. When a raven gets out of a cage it will never return. Also, when a raven flies from a ship in the middle of the ocean, it will always return to the ship. The meaning of the first is that once suchness has been resolved, one never returns to confusion. The meaning of the second is that this resolution generates the confidence that the thoughts that arise always return to the suchness of which they are the expression

These are the ten things that are necessary.

23 The Ten Unnecessary Things

Now we come to the ten things that are not necessary. First, when you realize directly that your mind is empty, hearing and contemplation are unnecessary. Realizing that is quite different from merely understanding it.

Second, when you recognize your awareness to be stainless, it is no longer necessary to purify wrongdoing.

Third, when you abide in the ultimate natural path, then the intentional gathering of the accumulations is no longer necessary, because you have attained or are attaining the result and essence of those accumulations.

Fourth, if you abide in the natural state through this having been pointed out and realized, it is not necessary to meditate using other methods.

Fifth, when you recognize thoughts as suchness, it is no longer necessary to meditate on nonthought or the absence of thought. It is no longer necessary to attempt to block thought.

Sixth, when the mental afflictions are recognized to be rootless and without basis, it is not necessary to rely upon their remedies.

Seventh, when all appearances and sounds are realized to be like magical illusions, it is no longer necessary to attempt to cause some to cease and to attempt to accomplish others. Since everything has been realized to be of one nature there is no preference or distinction between different phenomena.

Eighth, when suffering is recognized to be attainment or siddhi, it is unnecessary to search for pleasure.

Ninth, if the mind is realized to be unborn, it is unnecessary at the time of death for anyone to do *powa*, or the transference of consciousness.

Tenth, if everything you do with your body, speech, and mind is done for the benefit of others, there is no need to do anything more for your own benefit because the one is included in the other.

This list of ten things that are unnecessary is directed at those with the highest view and most perfect conduct: those who have actualized the qualities of the superior path.

24 The Ten Superior Things

Next are the ten things that are especially fine or noble. First, among the six different kinds of sentient beings, a human being possessing the freedoms and resources of a precious human existence is the most noble.

Second, among humans, most of whom have no connection with Dharma, an individual who practices Dharma is the most fine.

Third, among all the vehicles of the Buddhadharma, the ultimate essential vehicle, the true meaning, the mahamudra, is the most noble or fine.

Fourth, one instant of *sherab* or knowledge arising from meditation is superior to all of the knowledge that could arise from hearing and contemplation, because the whole point of hearing and contemplation is to lead to meditation and realization.

Fifth, one instant of noncomposite virtue, or virtue that is embraced by nonconceptuality of the doer, the recipient, and the action, is superior to all composite virtue, that is to say virtue performed for eons and eons with the concept of the inherent existence of the three aspects of a virtuous deed.

Sixth, one instant of nonconceptual samadhi is superior to all the conceptual samadhis that there are. This means that one instant of the ultimate completion stage, with a total lack of any kind of fixation whatsoever, is better than all the tranquility practices using different types of objects and, in the context of secret mantra, all the visualizations of deities, implements, letters, mantras, and so forth.

Seventh, one instant of undefiled virtue is superior to all the defiled virtue there is. Defiled virtue means a virtuous act performed with the motivation of accomplishing happiness or pleasure in this and future lives, the result of which is the maturation of that aim. Undefiled virtue means accomplishment of the virtue that leads to the attainments of arhats, bodhisattvas, and especially buddhas, that is, the attainments of superiors or aryas, because there are no defilements and no source of decay in their virtue.

This is related to the earlier point that compared composite virtue and noncomposite virtue. Both of these can be described as causes or as results. When composite and noncomposite virtue are compared as causes, composite virtue is virtue with conceptuality, and noncomposite virtue is virtue that transcends conceptual fixation. When compared as results, the result for composite virtue is the pleasures of samsara and for noncomposite virtue the attainment of buddhahood. In the present case, comparing defiled and undefiled virtue as cause, defiled virtue is performed with the motivation of accomplishing one's own pleasure and happiness, and undefiled virtue is performed with the motivation of accomplishing bodhicitta. The result in the case of defiled virtue is the pleasures of samsara, and in the case of undefiled virtue is awakening.

Eighth, one instant of realization is superior to all the experiences of meditation there could be. Experiences disappear and do not necessarily leave any effect upon us, whereas one instant of realization changes everything forever.

Ninth, one instant of nonconceptualized conduct is superior to all of the conceptually devised excellent conduct there could be. Although conduct within a conceptual framework—creating and setting up images of the body, speech, and mind of the buddhas, meditating conceptually upon deities, reciting mantras, and so forth—are of great merit, one instant of abiding in the state that transcends all elaboration is superior.

Finally, having no fixation on anything whatsoever is superior to all the material generosity there is. Although material generosity that is still embraced by the incorrect concept of an inherently existent person performing the generosity, and so forth, is of tremendous merit, it cannot match the recognition that there is no inherent existence, and the total absence of fixation that is generated by that recognition.

These are the ten especially fine or superior things.

25 The Ten Situations in Which Whatever Is Done Is Excellent

Next are the ten situations in which, no matter what you do, it is excellent. First, for those whose minds have totally gone to the Dharma, such that there is no thought of anything other than Dharma, if they abandon all mundane activity and abide only in retreat it is excellent; and if they do not abandon all mundane activities and do not abide in retreat it is also excellent. Because their minds have totally gone to the Dharma, such people are not prey to coarse mental afflictions.

Second, for those who have cut through all misconceptions in their own minds, if they meditate it is excellent, and if they do not meditate it is also excellent. Such people have resolved that the source of all suffering is the confusion that obscures the mind, and have recognized that the nature of the mind, which is otherwise obscured, is the spontaneously present dharmakaya.

Third, for those who have totally cut through all attachment or craving for pleasure, if they adopt a passionless existence, abandoning all mundane pleasures, it is excellent; and if they do not adopt a passionless existence, but abide in the midst of mundane pleasures, it is also excellent, because they have no attachment to such pleasures.

Fourth, for someone who has directly realized the nature of all things, it is excellent to live alone in an empty cave, and it is excellent to live as the leader of a vast community.

Fifth, for someone who has recognized that all appearances are like magical illusions, it is excellent to remain alone in an isolated retreat, and it is also excellent to travel around without direction through all lands.

Sixth, for those who have obtained complete control over their own minds, and therefore are not in any way afflicted by—or even affected by—thoughts and emotions, it is excellent if they abandon pleasurable sense experiences, and it is excellent if they enjoy them.

Seventh, for those who possess genuine bodhicitta, if they practice alone in solitude it is excellent, and if they abide in the midst of others, performing that which is beneficial to others, it is also excellent.

Eighth, for those who have unwavering devotion, such that no matter what occurs, or what conditions are present or not present, their devotion for their authentic teacher never increases or decreases but is always very, very strong, it is excellent if they live as attendants to their teacher, constantly in his or her presence; and it is fine if they do not.

Ninth, for those who have heard a lot of Dharma and have actually understood it, if signs of siddhi or attainment arise in their practice it is excellent, and if obstacles arise it is also excellent. Understanding the meaning of Dharma, they have no arrogance if signs arise and no fear if obstacles arise, because they recognize these both to be part of the path.

Tenth, for a yogi who has attained supreme realization, it is excellent if signs of common attainment arise, and it is also excellent if they do not. Common attainments are such things as extraordinary perception, the ability to bring others under our power, the ability to prolong our lives, the ability to heal ourselves of sickness, and so forth. These abilities are called "common" because they can occur for practitioners on the Buddhist path, and they can occur as well for people all over the world who generate them through a natural or acquired samadhi or meditative absorption. This is found commonly in India, for example. Supreme realization is the recognition that leads to awakening. For someone who has such an attainment, it does not matter whether or not he or she has the other.

These are the ten situations in which whatever someone does it is excellent.

26 The Ten Qualities of Genuine Dharma

Next come the ten qualities that are the blessings of Dharma being present in the world. The first of these is quite a long list. It includes the proclamation in the world of such things as the idea of the ten virtuous actions[23] to be practiced by all from the beginning; the idea of the six perfections to be practiced by intermediate practitioners; all the various presentations of emptiness from the hinayana, mahayana, and vajrayana points of view; the ideas of the thirty-seven factors of awakening and the four noble truths; the four *dhyanas*[24] and the four formless absorptions,[25] which are common and not only Buddhist; and especially the empowerments and instructions of the vajrayana. The presence of all of these things in the world is due to the blessings of the Dharma.

Second, within the human realm are high and great positions, such as royal families, and high and great stations within society, such as brahmins, and many powerful situations of wealth. Within the god realm are the six realms of desire gods such as the four great kings, the seventeen realms of form, the four formless realms, and so forth. The presence of all of these states of happiness in the world is due to the accumulation of merit by the individuals who experience them, and is therefore said to be a quality of, or due to the blessings of, the Dharma.

Third, the presence in the world of those who have attained any of the four levels of the path of the hearers—stream-enterers, one-time returners, non-returners, and arhats; the presence in the world of those attaining the levels of the pratyekabuddhas or solitary realizers; and the presence in the world of omniscient buddhas who have perfected the path of the mahayana, all arise because of the qualities of the Dharma.

Fourth, within the world is the effortless and spontaneously present accomplishment of benefit for sentient beings that occurs for as long as samsara is not empty, by means of the natural display of the compassion of buddhas in the form of the two form bodies. This is accomplished through the power of their original generation of the intention to attain supreme awakening and thereafter to establish all sentient beings in that state, and their aspiration during the path to perform activities through the form bodies that bring all sentient beings to happiness and awakening. The presence in the world of all this spontaneous activity is due to the qualities of the Dharma.

Fifth, all the abundant and excellent physical things that arise in the world to support, aid, and protect the lives of sentient beings arise through the power of the aspirations of bodhisattvas, and therefore through the qualities of the Dharma. The bodhisattvas make such aspirations as, "May I take the form of the four elements, and in the manner of each element support and protect all sentient beings."

Sixth, whatever slight happiness there is in the lower realms and in unrestful states arises from the virtuous merit accumulated by the beings in those states, and therefore arises through the qualities of the Dharma. The worst of the hell realms is *Avici* (or *narme* in Tibetan), the eighth hot hell, which is a state of uninterrupted suffering. From the point of view of Avici, the seventh hell and all the other ones above it are slightly better, in that there is slightly less suffering. The reason there is less suffering is that the sentient beings undergoing these experiences have slightly more virtue and slightly less wrongdoing in their mental continuums. Since it is through the power of virtue that there is the presence of comparative happiness, or less suffering, this arises through the qualities of Dharma.

Seventh, when an evil person turns his or her mind to Dharma and becomes a genuine and holy person who can be respected by everyone, this is an indication of the qualities of Dharma.

Eighth, when someone who has been carelessly engaging in such wrongdoing that it produces future fuel for the fires of hell, turns his or her mind towards the Dharma, and comes to bring about the experience of higher realms and liberation, this indicates the qualities of Dharma.

Ninth, when someone merely has faith, interest, or delight in Dharma, or merely takes on the appearance or the costume of a practitioner, and yet by this alone becomes pleasing to everyone and an object of people's respect, this indicates the qualities of Dharma.

Finally, when someone abandons all possessions and leaves the world for a state of homelessness, living in isolated retreat, and yet spontaneously finds abundant and excellent sustenance, this is a quality of the Dharma.

These ten things are the briefest possible summation of the boundless qualities of Dharma.

27 The Ten Things That Are Merely Names

Next are the ten things that are merely names. First, since the nature of the ground cannot be explained or demonstrated, *ground* is just a name. The nature of the ground of experience is beyond all elaboration, and therefore cannot be communicated. Therefore, any name or term applied to it is just something designating it and does not really describe it.

Second, since the path is not a composite phenomenon and is therefore not something that can be divided into a traveler and traveling, *path* is just a name.

Third, in the ultimate nature there is nothing to see and no viewer, so *realization* is just a name. When we say realization, we think of something new being seen, but there is not anything to see and there is not anyone seeing it.

Fourth, in naturalness or uncontrivance, there is nothing to meditate on and no doing of meditation, so the *experience of meditation* is just a name.

Fifth, in the ultimate nature there is no arising, cessation, or abiding, and therefore there is nothing to be done and no process of conduct, so *conduct* is just a name.

Sixth, since the ultimate nature of all things is free of any kind of elaboration or distinction and is not a composite, and therefore there is nothing to be guarded and no guarding, the term *samaya* is merely a name or convention.

Seventh, ultimately there is nothing to be accumulated or added, and no accumulation, so *the two accumulations* is merely a name.

Eighth, since ultimately there is nothing to be purified and no purification, *the two obscurations*—the cognitive and afflictive obscurations—are just names.

Ninth, ultimately there is nothing to be abandoned and no process of abandonment, so *samsara* is just a name.

Tenth, ultimately there is nothing to be attained and no attainment, since the fruition is spontaneously present as our true nature, so *fruition* is just a name. As long as we are still under the power of the habitual patterns of confusion, however, interdependence and the results of actions are valid and unfailing. For example, while we are asleep and dreaming, we still are frightened, pleased, and so forth by the appearances that arise in the dream; but when we wake up, all of the images of the dream have no further validity and are of no value. In the same way, just as the appearances are valid in the dream, so is the interdependent nature by which our confused experience is characterized.

This list of ten things that are mere names is therefore concerned with a very high level of realization, as was the case with some earlier sections. This kind of thing, if misunderstood, might lead you to perform negative actions, such as in the earlier story of the person who killed a goat.

28 The Ten Things That Are Spontaneously Present as Great Bliss

Next come the ten instances of spontaneously present great bliss. First, since the nature of the mind of each and every sentient being abides as the dharmakaya, it is spontaneously present as great bliss, and therefore the dharmakaya or great bliss does not have to be newly created or added.

Second, since there is nothing in the phenomenal world that passes beyond the expanse of the nature or the ground of all things, the ground is spontaneously present as great bliss.

Third, since the realization that transcends conceptual mind and is beyond the extremes of nihilism and the assertion of permanence, is without the elaborations of partiality and distinction, it is spontaneously present as great bliss.

Fourth, since the experience of nonactivity in the mind transcends the elaboration of conceptuality, it is spontaneously present as great bliss.

Fifth, since the conduct that is effortless and beyond conceptually designated activity transcends the elaboration of acceptance and rejection, it is spontaneously present as great bliss.

Sixth, since there are not the elaborations of grasped objects and a grasping subject in the dharmakaya, which is the unity of the expanse of emptiness and the ultimate wisdom that is the cognition of emptiness, the dharmakaya is spontaneously present as great bliss.

Seventh, since the sambhogakaya, which is self-arisen compassion, does not possess the elaborations of birth and death, it is spontaneously present as great bliss.

Eighth, since the nirmanakaya, which is self-arising compassion, transcends the elaboration of the false imputation of an inherent duality to experience, it is spontaneously present as great bliss.

Ninth, since all the various turnings of the wheel of Dharma by the Buddha transcend the elaboration of the false imputation of an inherently existent self, they are spontaneously present as great bliss.

Finally, since the activity of unlimited compassion has no divisions and no time frame, it is spontaneously present as great bliss.

These are the ten instances of spontaneously present great bliss.

Conclusion

That then is the meaning of *A Precious Garland of the Supreme Path* by the incomparable Dagpo Rinpoche, starting with the ten causes of loss and ending with the ten things that are spontaneously present as great bliss. All stages of the path, from the recognition of having attained the precious human existence up to the causes, conditions, nature, and qualities of supreme awakening, and the essence of all the presentations of the Buddha's teachings, both those of sutra and those of tantra, have been explained in this text. These teachings are not simply Gampopa's own random composition, but are the expression of his genuine realization which arose from his thorough practice, based on the complete instruction received from lamas who were absolutely authentic and realized themselves.

In this text is contained the essence of the teachings that Gampopa received from his kind gurus of the Kadampa tradition, which is the stainless transmission of the words and instructions of the glorious Atisha and his lineage, such as Geshe Dromtönpa, Geshe Chengawa, and so forth. Atisha, as Gampopa remarks in the text, was dispatched to Tibet and appointed as the regent for Tibet by both his main root guru, who was known as Lord Serlingpa (which means "the one from Indonesia"), and his yidam, Arya Tara.

This text also contains the essence of the stainless speech that Gampopa received from the king of all venerable ones, Lord Milarepa, who held the essence of the minds of all the scholars and siddhas of India, as had been transmitted by Lord Marpa. Marpa relied upon innumerable teachers, but principally those as famous in India at that time as the sun and moon themselves, the supreme beings Naropa and Maitripa.

Thus, the essences of these two traditions have been combined in the form of this text, *A Precious Garland of the Supreme Path*. This was done by Lord Sonam Rinchen—Gampopa—who held the treasury of the instructions of the Kadampa coming from Serlingpa and Atisha, and the mahamudra lineage coming from Naropa, Maitripa, Marpa, and so on.

It was said by Lord Gampopa, "For all individuals of the future who have devotion for me and who are depressed because they cannot meet me, if they will look at the texts composed by me, such as *A Precious Garland of the Supreme Path* and *The Jewel Ornament of Liberation*, then it will be exactly the same as meeting me." Therefore, all those who are fortunate enough to have devotion for Gampopa should be diligent in the use of these two treatises. Gampopa composed these two texts not so much for the benefit of the time in which he was living but for the benefit of those who would come in the future, and specifically for the benefit of those who would be practicing the tradition that comes from him. That means no one other than ourselves.

Further, in general it is said that if you pray to any guru of the lineage of transmission of the mahamudra, by receiving his or her blessing you will attain realization, and whatever realization you have will increase, but this is said to be especially true in the case of Lord Gampopa. He is to such an extent the embodiment of mahamudra that merely to think of him with any degree of devotion will spark realization in those who do not have it and increase realization instantly in those who do.

In this sense Gampopa is quite special. These two texts are his most famous works, and they are, as he said, the embodiment of all his compassion, all his wisdom, and all his ability to transmit the realization of mahamudra.

For a very short period of time we have studied the comparatively brief words that make up this text. I sincerely ask you please not to leave this text as mere words in your memory, but to hold the meaning of it and partake of the splendor of it with all the insight, all the diligence, and all the devotion you can muster. Because of the blessings of Lord Gampopa, if you do this, there is no doubt that you will attain buddhahood.

QUESTIONS AND ANSWERS

Q: The sixth point of the ten situations in which no matter what you do it is excellent was that for someone who has attained complete control over the mind and who is not afflicted by thoughts or emotions, it is excellent either to abandon sense experiences or to enjoy them. I have been very confused by rumors and gossip about certain teachers who are deemed great, who have enjoyed sense experiences in a way that tends to go against the vows and samaya. How do we deal with that confusion or regard that?

A: At this point we have absolutely no way to determine what is going on in the mind of anyone else, so there is no point in trying to determine whether what someone is doing is really a defect or not. All we can do is determine whether we have defects. In the case of teachers whose conduct you find disturbing, the best way to deal with it is to have total faith, because if there is something wrong it will not harm you, and if there is not something wrong, the more faith you have the better. If you cannot do that, you should at least hope for the best and not judge them so severely that there is no possibility of developing any faith later on.

The trouble is that many siddhas and bodhisattvas of the past have acted in really strange ways, which under any other circumstance would be totally immoral, because specific sentient beings needed specific actions. For example, Tilopa, whom we accept as enlightened, killed a lot of fish. Now, there is normally nothing worse than killing, but Tilopa had the ability to liberate those sentient beings and bring them to a higher state of existence. There would have been no way to tell that at the time.

Q: Some practitioners know what will happen after death. How do we know the signs indicating that we can certainly be reborn in the pure land or become a buddha?

A: Through practice. Especially, if you can get to the point that you have not so much as a hair's tip of attachment to the pleasures of this life, to any places, people, or things, or even to your own body, then you will have confidence that when you die you can be reborn in the pure land. This confidence, which is the same thing I spoke of earlier, grows with practice. The more you practice, the more confidence you will have.

Q: We spend eight hours sleeping without practicing Dharma. I think that is a waste of time. What can we do to practice Dharma during sleep?

A: There are ways of doing this. Among the fifty-one mental factors described in the abhidharma, there are four that can be virtuous, nonvirtuous, or neutral. These are sleep, examination, understanding, and remorse. Whether your sleep is positive, negative, or neutral depends largely upon your attitude when you go to sleep. That is the most important thing. For example, if you go to sleep in a state of stupidity in which you are not thinking of anything, but are just groggy, then the sleep becomes pure stupidity. If you go to sleep angry, your sleep will be filled with anger, and if you go to sleep in a virtuous frame of mind, your sleep will be turned to virtue.

It is recommended that before you go to sleep you perform the self-visualization of Chenrezig or Amitabha and recite the mantra very quietly and slowly, maintaining the visualization and reciting the mantra, and then relaxing and slowing down the recitation of mantra as you go to sleep. If you have confidence in this process, it will work and it will transform your sleep. The sign of this is that every time you wake up in the middle of the night, you will find yourself saying the mantra. If you apply mindfulness in such a way, it is definitely possible for sleep not to be a waste of time.

Q: Of the two accumulations, the accumulation of wisdom and the accumulation of merit, is either one more important than the other, or are they both equally important?

A: We could say that merely from the point of view of their names, wisdom is somehow better or more important than merit. Ultimately speaking, though, in the accomplishment of buddhahood they are equally necessary. They are somewhat like the two wings of a bird. Specifically, in the accomplishment of dharmakaya, which is the abandonment of all defects and the ultimate benefit for oneself, the principal element is the accumulation of wisdom. In the accomplishment of the form bodies, which are the complete, continuous, and spontaneous performance of the ultimate benefit for others, the main thing is the accumulation of merit.

Q: Of the ten bewilderments, I believe the third one was not to be content with what we have today but to make plans for the future, and I would like some clarification. Does this refer to practice, or is it in a material sense, such as saving money for our retirement? Also, is there a contradiction here with what Gampopa says elsewhere, that we should be concerned about our future lives?

A: There is no contradiction, because when you are instructed to shorten your attitude and only think of the present, it means not to make plans in a mundane or worldly sense, not to count on what cannot be counted on; and in fact, it means to think that you might die at any moment. You should shorten your attitude with respect to mundane things, not with respect to Dharma.

With respect to Dharma, you should lengthen your attitude. You should recognize that you might be dead at any moment and therefore you should consider what will happen after death; you should consider the results of actions, and so forth. Especially if you have generated bodhicitta, you should even make aspirations for very far in the future, thinking, "When I am a bodhisattva, may I perform such and such vast types of benefit for sentient beings," and so forth. Thus you should shorten your attitude with respect to mundane things, and lengthen it with respect to the Dharma.

The Root Text

THE INSTRUCTIONS OF GAMPOPA: A PRECIOUS GARLAND OF THE SUPREME PATH

Translated by Lama Yeshe Gyamtso and Laura M. Roth

Namo ratna guru. To those who liberate beings from the terrifying ocean of samsara that is so hard to cross, who are adorned with the pure practice of the precious Kagyu, whose river of blessings is inexhaustible like the expanse of an ocean; to the holy gurus of the stainless practice lineage of vast, far-seeing, spontaneously accomplished aspirations, I pay homage and go for refuge. I pray that you engulf me with your splendor.

Having considered for a long time the oral tradition that has come from those Kagyus, I will write down a precious garland of the supreme path, instructions that are extremely valuable to those fortunate ones who directly or indirectly venerate me.

1*

Those individuals wishing to attain liberation and omniscient buddhahood should, from the beginning, recollect the ten causes of loss:

This pure human body, so difficult to acquire, is lost in wrong-doing. [4]

This pure human body with its freedom and resources, so difficult to possess, is lost in ordinary physical death without Dharma.

This brief human life in the age of decadence is lost and used up in meaningless activities.

This mind whose nature is the dharmakaya, beyond elaboration, is lost and mired in the swamp of samsaric confusion.

The holy guru who leads one on the path is lost if one is separate from him at any time until one attains awakening.

Vows and samaya, the ship of liberation, are lost in destruction by *kleshas*, carelessness, and adverse conditions.

The experience and realization that one has acquired through the intercession of one's guru are lost in the forest of mental formations.

The profound instructions of siddhas are lost by being sold to the unworthy.

Sentient beings, one's kind parents, are lost when one abandons them through anger.

One's youthful three gates are lost in ordinary indifference.[5]

Those are the ten causes of loss.

* Note: The numbers at the beginning of each section indicate the corresponding chapter of Khenpo Karthar Rinpoche's commentary. The numbers in brackets indicate the corresponding page number of the Tibetan text.

2

These are the ten necessary things:

It is necessary to be independent so that one is not misled by advice.

It is necessary to practice with faith and diligence in accordance with the instructions of the holy guru.

It is necessary to select instructions of one's guru unmistakenly, through understanding the difference between instructions that are appropriate and inappropriate.

It is necessary to enact the intentions of the holy guru with knowledge, faith, and diligence.

It is necessary that through one's possession of mindfulness, attentiveness, and carefulness, one's three gates be unobscured by defects.

It is necessary that one be stable and independent in one's practice, through possessing courage and the armor of diligence.

It is necessary that, by being without attachment and craving, one avoid giving one's nose-rope to others.

It is necessary to be diligent in the continual gathering of the two accumulations, by complementing one's practice with preparation, execution, and conclusion.

It is necessary that one turn one's mind to benefiting beings, both directly and indirectly, with loving-kindness and compassion. [6]

It is necessary that through knowledge, understanding, and realization, one not mistake all things to be substantial and inherently endowed with characteristics.

Those are the ten necessary things.

3

These are the ten things upon which to rely:

Rely upon a holy guru who possesses realization and compassion.

Rely upon solitude that is isolated, pleasant, and endowed with blessing.
Rely upon stable companions of like views and practice.
Rely upon moderation, recollecting the defects of necessities.
Rely impartially upon the instructions of the lineage of siddhas.
Rely upon materials, medicines, mantras, and profound interdependence that are beneficial to oneself and others.
Rely upon food that suits your constitution, and upon the path of method.
Rely upon Dharma and conduct that benefit your experience.
Rely upon worthy disciples who have faith and respect.
Rely upon mindfulness and attentiveness throughout the four modes of conduct.
Those are the ten things upon which to rely.

4

These are the ten things to be abandoned:
Abandon masters whose every action is mixed with the eight worldly dharmas. [7]
Abandon retinue and negative companions that harm your mind and experience.
Abandon places and hermitages of great distraction and danger.
Abandon sustenance obtained through theft, robbery, and deception.
Abandon actions and activities that harm your mind and your experience.
Abandon food and conduct that harm your constitution.
Abandon fixation and attachment that bind you in desire, hope, and greed.
Abandon careless conduct that causes others to lose faith.
Abandon meaningless walking and sitting around.

Abandon concealing your own defects and proclaiming the defects of others.
Those are the ten things to be abandoned.

5

These are the ten things not to be abandoned:
Since compassion is the root of benefit for others, do not abandon it.
Since appearances are the radiance of the mind, do not abandon them.
Since thoughts are the play of *dharmata*, do not abandon them.
Since kleshas are the revelation of wisdom, do not abandon them.
Since desirable things are the water and manure of experience and realization, do not abandon them. [8]
Since sickness and suffering are teachers, do not abandon them.
Since enemies and obstructers are the exhortation of dharmata, do not abandon them. If they disappear spontaneously, that is siddhi. Do not reject that.
Since the path of method is always a support for the path of knowledge, do not abandon it.
Do not abandon physical Dharma practices that you can accomplish.
Do not abandon the intention to benefit others, even though you have little ability.
Those are the ten things not to be abandoned.

6

These are the ten things to be known:
Since external appearances are confusion, know them to be unreal.
Since the internal mind itself is without a self, know it to be empty.

Since the thoughts in between arise conditionally, know them to be adventitious.
Since this body and speech, composed of the elements, are composite, know them to be impermanent.
Since all the pleasure and suffering of sentient beings arises from karma, know the results of actions to be unfailing.
Since suffering is a cause of renunciation, know it to be a teacher. [9]
Since pleasure and comfort are the root of samsara, know craving and attachment to be Mara.
Since distractions are conditions unconducive to the accumulation of merit, know them to be obstacles.
Since obstacles are exhortations for the virtuous, know enemies and obstructers to be your gurus.
Since, in absolute truth, all things are without a nature, know everything to be the same.
Those are the ten things to be known.

7

These are the ten things to be practiced:
Having entered the gate of Dharma, do not enter the herd-like concerns of people; practice in accordance with Dharma.
Having abandoned your birthplace, do not establish yourself in human lands; practice without attachment.
Relying upon a holy guru, abandon arrogance; practice in accordance with his or her instructions.
Having trained your mind through hearing and reflection, do not just teach; practice what you have learned.
When realization has arisen in you, do not be satisfied with it; practice without distraction. [10]
When practice has arisen within you, do not enter into the distractions of communities; practice.
Having promised and committed yourself, do not be careless with your three gates; practice the three trainings.

Having generated the mind of supreme awakening, do not accomplish benefit for yourself; perform all practice for the benefit of others.
Having entered the gate of mantra, do not leave your three gates in the ordinary state; practice cultivating them as the three mandalas.
While young, do not travel meaninglessly; practice austerities in the presence of a holy teacher.
Those are the ten things to be practiced.

8

These are the ten things to emphasize:
Beginners should emphasize hearing and reflection.
When experience has arisen, emphasize meditation practice.
Until you attain stability, emphasize solitude.
If excitement predominates, emphasize the subduing of awareness.
If torpor and depression predominate, emphasize the expansion of awareness.
Until your mind is stable, emphasize even placement.
When even placement has been stabilized, emphasize subsequent attainment.[26] [11]
If unconducive conditions are many, emphasize threefold patience.
If desire, hope, attachment, and craving are great, emphasize forceful renunciation.
If love and compassion are weak, emphasize the cultivation of bodhicitta.
Those are the ten things to emphasize.

9

These are the ten exhortations:
Contemplating the difficulty of acquiring these freedoms and resources, exhort yourself to practice genuine Dharma.

Contemplating death and impermanence, exhort yourself to cultivate virtue.
Contemplating the unfailing results of actions, exhort yourself to abandon wrongdoing.
Contemplating the defects of samsara, exhort yourself to accomplish liberation.
Contemplating the sufferings of samsaric beings, exhort yourself to cultivate bodhicitta.
Contemplating the mistaken confusion of sentient beings, exhort yourself to hear and reflect.
Contemplating the difficulty of abandoning the habits of confusion, exhort yourself to practice meditation. [12]
Contemplating the virulence of kleshas in this age of decadence, exhort yourself to apply their remedies.
Contemplating the many unconducive conditions present in this age of decadence, exhort yourself to be patient.
Contemplating the empty waste of a human life spent in various distractions, exhort yourself to be diligent.
Those are the ten exhortations.

10

These are the ten deviations:
If you have little faith and much knowledge, that is the deviation of becoming a talker.
If you have much faith and little knowledge, that is the deviation of pointless exertion.
If you have much fortitude and no instructions, that is the deviation of defects and sidetracks.
If you have not previously eliminated your superimpositions[27] with hearing and reflection, that is the deviation of meditation upon obscurity.
If fresh understanding is not applied in practice, that is the deviation of becoming a jaded Dharma expert.
If your mind is untrained in method—great compassion—that is the deviation into the path of the lesser vehicle.

If your mind is untrained in knowledge—emptiness—that is the deviation into the path of samsara. [13]
If the eight worldly dharmas are not overcome, that is the deviation of whatever you do becoming a worldly decoration.
If townsfolk have too much faith and interest in you, that is the deviation of having to please ordinary people.
If you have great qualities and power, but an unstable mind, that is the deviation of becoming a performer of village rituals.
Those are the ten deviations.

11

These are the ten confusions of one thing for another:
There is confusion between faith and desire.
There is confusion between loving compassion and attachment.
There is confusion between the emptiness that is the nature of all knowables and the emptiness that is intellectually posited.
There is confusion between the *dharmadhatu* and the view of annihilation.
There is confusion between experience and realization.
There is confusion between virtuous people and deceptive people.
There is confusion between someone who has eradicated bewilderment and someone who has been carried off by Mara.
There is confusion between siddhas and charlatans.
There is confusion between benefiting others and benefiting oneself.
There is confusion between skillful methods and deception.
Those are the ten confusions of one thing for another.

12

These are the ten unmistaken things:

To leave home without attachment to anything, to take ordination and be homeless, is unmistaken. [14]

To carry the holy guru, one's teacher, on top of one's head like the cloth that binds one's topknot, is unmistaken.

To combine the hearing, reflection, and meditation aspects of Dharma is unmistaken.

To have a high view and modest conduct is unmistaken.

To have an open mind and strict commitment is unmistaken.

To have much knowledge and little pride is unmistaken.

To be rich in instruction and diligent in practice is unmistaken.

To have good experience and realization and no arrogance or vanity is unmistaken.

To be independent in solitude and harmonious in company is unmistaken.

To be without attachment to one's own benefit and skillful in benefiting others is unmistaken.

Those are the ten unmistaken things.

13

These are the fourteen useless things:

Having acquired a human body, not to recollect genuine Dharma is like returning empty-handed from an island of jewels, and is useless.

Having entered the gate of Dharma, to lead a worldly life is like a moth flying into a lamp flame, and is useless.

For someone with no faith to abide in the presence of a great teacher of Dharma is like dying of thirst on the shore of an ocean, and is useless. [15]

Dharma that does not remedy the four roots and fixation on a self is like an ax placed beside a tree, and is useless.

Instructions that do not remedy the kleshas are like bags of medicine carried about by an ill person, and are useless.

Training the tongue in words whose meaning has not entered one's mind is like the recitations of a parrot, and is useless.

To take by stealth, banditry, and deception that which has not been given to one, and subsequently give it away, is like washing sheepskin in water, and is useless.

To harm sentient beings and then offer them to the Three Jewels is like cutting off a child's flesh and offering it to its mother, and is useless.

To undertake deception and patience in order to benefit oneself in this life is like a cat stalking a mouse, and is useless.

To perform great acts of virtue with the wish of acquiring fame and service in this life is like exchanging a wish-fulfilling jewel for a morsel of food, and is useless. [16]

To have heard much and yet have an ordinary mind is like a physician struck down by illness, and is useless.

To be learned in instruction and have no experience is like a treasury of riches to which there is no key, and is useless.

To teach Dharma without having realized it oneself is like the sightless leading the sightless, and is useless.

To hold experiences arising from methods to be supreme, and not to search for the true nature of things, is like taking brass to be gold, and is useless.

Those are the fourteen useless things.

14

These are the eighteen hidden evils of practitioners:

To abide in solitude and accomplish greatness in this life is a hidden evil of practitioners.

To lead a community and accomplish one's own desires is a hidden evil of practitioners.

To be learned in Dharma and not avoid wrongdoing is a hidden evil of practitioners.
To possess many instructions and leave one's mind ordinary is a hidden evil of practitioners.
To have virtuous moral conduct and great desire is a hidden evil of practitioners. [17]
To have good experience and realization and an untamed mind is a hidden evil of practitioners.
To enter the gate of Dharma and not abandon the attachment and aversion of human affairs is a hidden evil of practitioners.
To abandon human affairs and cultivate divine Dharma but subsequently return to farming is a hidden evil of practitioners.
To understand the meaning and not practice it is a hidden evil of practitioners.
To make a commitment to practice and not fulfill it is a hidden evil of practitioners.
To have nothing to do other than Dharma and yet not ameliorate one's conduct is a hidden evil of practitioners.
To worry about acquiring food and clothing, even though they arise spontaneously, is a hidden evil of practitioners.
To devote the power arising from one's virtuous endeavors entirely to the healing of the sick and the prevention of *si* is a hidden evil of practitioners.
To teach profound instructions in order to acquire food and wealth is a hidden evil of practitioners.
To indirectly praise oneself and denigrate others is a hidden evil of practitioners.
To present instructions to others while one's own mind is contrary to Dharma is a hidden evil of practitioners.
To be unable to live in solitude and unaware of how to be with people is a hidden evil of practitioners. [18]
To be unable to support happiness and withstand suffering is a hidden evil of practitioners.
Those are the eighteen hidden evils of practitioners.

15

These are the twelve indispensable things:
From the beginning, the faith arising from deep fear of birth and death is indispensable.
A guru who leads one on the path of liberation is indispensable.
Knowledge, an understanding of the meaning, is indispensable.
Diligence, courageous and armor-like, is indispensable.
Cultivation, without complacency, of the three trainings and the two accumulations is indispensable.
A view that realizes the nature of all knowables is indispensable.
Meditation in which the mind itself abides wherever it is placed is indispensable.
Conduct in which one takes all one's actions on the path is indispensable.
Practice of instructions—without leaving them as mere words—for transcending adverse conditions, obstructors, maras, and deviations are indispensable. [19]
Great confidence, a happy mind at the time of the separation of body and mind, is indispensable.
A result, the spontaneous manifestation within one of the *trikaya*, is indispensable.
Those are the twelve indispensable things.

16

These are the eleven marks of a holy person:
It is a mark of a holy person to have little jealousy and pride.
It is a mark of a holy person to have little desire and to be content with meager possessions.
It is a mark of a holy person to be without haughtiness, vanity, and arrogance.
It is a mark of a holy person to be without deception and pretense.

It is a mark of a holy person to examine any action with alertness and to perform it with alert mindfulness.
It is a mark of a holy person to attend to the results of actions as carefully as one protects the pupils of one's eyes.
It is a mark of a holy person to be without pretense with regard to vows and samaya.
It is a mark of a holy person to be without preference and infatuation toward sentient beings.
It is a mark of a holy person not to be angered by the wrong-doing of others, but to have patience. [20]
It is a mark of a holy person to give all victory to other people and accept all defeat oneself.
It is a mark of a holy person to be unlike worldly people in all thoughts and conduct.
Those are the eleven marks of a holy person. Their opposites are the marks of an unholy person.

17

These are the ten things of no benefit:
Since no matter how much service and attention you pay to your illusory body, it is impermanent and certain to be destroyed, there is no benefit.
Since no matter how much greed and avarice you have for possessions and wealth, you will die naked and with empty hands, there is no benefit.
Since no matter how much trouble you go to in the construction of castles and mansions, you will die alone and your corpse will be put out the door, there is no benefit.
Since no matter how many things you lovingly give your children, nephews, and nieces, on the day of your death they will not have an instant's power to help you, there is no benefit. [21]
Since no matter how much attention and concern you lavish on family and friends, you will die alone without their company, there is no benefit.

Since even if you have many children, nephews and nieces, they are impermanent, and it is therefore certain that the things you give them will be abandoned, there is no benefit.

Since no matter how much effort you put into the acquisition of property and authority and its execution, on the day of your death your connection with your region will cease, there is no benefit.

Since, having entered the gate of Dharma through faith, if you do not conduct yourself in accordance with Dharma it will cause lower migrations, there is no benefit.

Since, no matter how much Dharma you know, having trained your mind in hearing and reflection, if it is not practiced you will have nothing by which to take death onto the path, there will be no benefit.

Since even if you remain for a long time in the presence of a holy teacher, if you have no faith and respect you will not receive his qualities or blessing, there is no benefit.

Those are the ten things of no benefit.

18

These are the ten ways of accomplishing one's own disaster: [22]

When a single person marries it is like a fool eating virulent poison, and is the purchase of one's own disaster.

Wrongdoing devoid of Dharma is like a lunatic leaping into an abyss, and is accomplishing one's own disaster.

Deceiving others with charlatanism is like serving poisoned food, and accomplishes one's own disaster.

For someone of little intelligence to lead people is like an old woman guarding cattle, and is the accomplishment of one's own disaster.

To exert oneself in benefiting oneself, motivated by the eight worldly dharmas, rather than exerting oneself in benefiting others through an excellent motivation, is like a sightless person wandering the northern steppes, and is accomplishing one's own disaster.

Undertaking a great endeavor that one cannot accomplish is like a weak person trying to carry a heavy burden, and is accomplishing one's own disaster.

Disregarding through pride one's holy guru and the Victor's teachings is like a rash ruler ignoring his council, and is accomplishing one's own disaster.

Deferring practice and wandering through the communities of ordinary people is like a wild animal wandering into an inhabited valley, and is accomplishing one's own disaster. [23]

Not fostering natural wisdom, but being disturbed by the elaborations of distractions, is like a *garuda* breaking its wings, and is accomplishing one's own disaster.

Carelessly consuming the property of the guru and the Three Jewels is like a small child cramming embers into its mouth, and is accomplishing one's own disaster.

Those are the ten ways of accomplishing one's own disaster.

19

These are the ten things that are great kindnesses to oneself:

To abandon the attachment and aversion of human affairs and practice divine Dharma is a great kindness to oneself.

To abandon cohabitation and companionship, and to rely upon holy persons, is a great kindness to oneself.

To abandon activities of distraction and cultivate hearing, reflection, and meditation, is a great kindness to oneself.

To abandon familiarity with villagers and live alone in solitude is a great kindness to oneself.

To cut through the entanglements of desirable things, and remain independent and without attachment, is a great kindness to oneself.

To be content with meager things and have no desire for or interest in fine things is a great kindness to oneself.

Not to surrender one's freedom to others, but to stabilize one's practice, is a great kindness to oneself. [24]

Not to look toward the immediate pleasures of this life, but to accomplish the permanent pleasure of awakening, is a great kindness to oneself.

To abandon fixation on the reality of things and to cultivate emptiness is a great kindness to oneself.

Not leaving one's three gates in the ordinary state but endeavoring to unify the two accumulations is a great kindness to oneself.

Those are the ten things that are great kindnesses to oneself.

20

These are the ten perfect things:

Trusting in the results of actions is the perfect view for one of lesser capacity.

Realizing that all external and internal dharmas are the four unities[28]—appearance and emptiness, awareness and emptiness—is the perfect view for one of intermediate capacity.

Realizing that the viewed, the viewer, and the realization are indivisible is the perfect view for one of the highest capacity.

To abide one-pointedly on the object is the perfect meditation for one of lesser capacity.

To abide in the *samadhi* of the four unities is the perfect meditation for one of intermediate capacity.

To abide without concept in the indivisibility of meditated, meditator, and practice is the perfect meditation for one of the highest capacity. [25]

Guarding the results of actions like the pupils of one's eyes is the perfect conduct for one of lesser capacity.

Experiencing all dharmas as like dreams and illusions is the perfect conduct for one of intermediate capacity.

Being without any conduct whatsoever is the perfect conduct for one of the highest capacity.
Lessening and pacifying all kleshas and the fixation on a self is the perfect sign of progress for those of the highest, intermediate, or lesser capacity.
Those are the ten perfect things.

21

These are the ten bewilderments of practitioners:
Not relying upon a guru who properly practices genuine Dharma, but following a smooth-talking charlatan, is extremely bewildered.
Not searching out the instructions of the siddhas' oral lineage but earnestly emphasizing pointless intellectual Dharma is extremely bewildered.
Not to pass one's human life in contentment with whatever appearances arise at the moment, but to make elaborate plans based on the assumption that things will remain the same, is extremely bewildered. [26]
Not to reflect upon the meaning of Dharma while living alone, but to teach Dharma amidst an extensive retinue, is extremely bewildered.
Not to use excess possessions for offerings and generosity, but to accumulate wealth and belongings with greed and through deception, is extremely bewildered.
Not properly guarding one's samaya and vows but carelessly letting go of one's three gates is extremely bewildered.
Not familiarizing oneself with realization of the true nature of things, but using up one's life with various unimportant activities, is extremely bewildered.
Not taming one's own confusion, but rashly and foolishly attempting to tame the minds of others, is extremely bewildered.

Not fostering the experience that is born in one's mind, but cultivating ways to achieve greatness in this life, is extremely bewildered.

Now, when auspicious conditions are assembled, not engaging in diligence but delighting in indolence is extremely bewildered.

Those are the ten bewilderments of practitioners.

22

These are the ten necessary things:

In the beginning, genuine faith arising from fear of birth and death is necessary, like the attitude of a deer that has fled from a trap. [27]

In the middle stage, diligence such that one has no regret at one's death is necessary, like the attitude of a farmer at the harvest.

In the end, a happy mind that cannot die is necessary, like the attitude of a person who has completed a great endeavor.

In the beginning, a recognition of urgency is necessary, like that of someone pierced by an arrow.

In the middle stage, undistracted meditation is necessary, like the intense feelings of a mother whose only child has died.

In the end, a recognition that there is nothing to do is necessary, like the attitude of cattle freed by rustlers.

In the beginning, the generation of certainty toward Dharma is necessary, like the feeling of a hungry person who encounters good food.

In the middle stage, the generation of certainty toward one's own mind is necessary, like the attitude of the wrestler who acquired the jewel.

In the end, the generation of certainty toward nonduality is necessary, like the exposure of an impostor's deception.

The resolution of suchness is necessary, like a raven flying from a ship.
Those are the ten necessary things.

23

These are the ten unnecessary things:
If the mind itself is realized to be empty, hearing and reflection are unnecessary. [28]
If awareness is recognized to be stainless, the purification of wrongdoing is unnecessary.
If one abides on the natural path, gathering the accumulations is unnecessary.
If one cultivates the natural state, meditation upon the path of method is unnecessary.
If one recognizes thoughts to be *dharmata*, nonconceptual meditation is unnecessary.
If the kleshas are recognized to be rootless, reliance upon remedies is unnecessary.
If appearances and sounds are recognized as illusory, rejection and creation are unnecessary.
If suffering is recognized to be *siddhi*, searching for pleasure is unnecessary.
If one's own mind is realized to be unborn, transference is unnecessary.
If everything one does is for the benefit of others, the accomplishment of one's own benefit is unnecessary.
Those are the ten unnecessary things.

24

These are the ten superior things:
One human body endowed with freedoms and resources is superior to all other sentient beings of the six types.

One person endowed with Dharma is superior to all ordinary people lacking Dharma.
This vehicle of the essential meaning is superior to the paths of all other vehicles. [29]
One instant of knowledge arising from meditation is superior to all knowledge arising from hearing and reflection.
One instant of noncomposite virtue is superior to all the composite virtues that there are.
One instant of nonconceptual samadhi is superior to all the conceptual samadhis that there are.
One instant of undefiled virtue is superior to all the defiled virtues that there are.
The arising of one instant of realization is superior to all the experiences that arise in one's mind.
One instant of unselfconscious conduct is superior to all the self-conscious virtuous conduct that there is.
Being without fixation on anything whatsoever is superior to all the material generosity that there is.
Those are the ten superior things.

25

These are the ten situations in which whatever is done is excellent: [30]
If an individual whose mind has gone to Dharma abandons activities, it is excellent. If he or she does not abandon them, it is also excellent.
If an individual who has cut through superimpositions in the mind meditates, it is excellent. If he or she does not meditate, it is also excellent.
If an individual who has cut through entanglement in desirable things acts without passion, it is excellent. If he or she does not act that way, it is also excellent.

If an individual who has directly realized dharmata sleeps in an empty cave, it is excellent. If he or she leads a large community, it is also excellent.

If an individual who recognizes appearances to be illusory lives alone in retreat, it is excellent. If he or she wanders throughout the land, it is also excellent.

If an individual who has attained freedom of mind abandons desirable things, it is excellent. If he or she partakes of them, it is also excellent.

If an individual endowed with bodhicitta practices in solitude, it is excellent. If he or she benefits others in a community, it is also excellent.

If an individual whose devotion is unfluctuating remains in the presence of his or her guru, it is excellent. If he or she does not remain there, it is also excellent.

If, for an individual who has heard much and understood the meaning of what he or she has heard, siddhi arise, it is excellent. [31] If obstacles arise, it is also excellent.

If a yogi who has attained supreme realization possesses signs of common siddhi, it is excellent. If he or she does not possess them, it is also excellent.

Those are the ten situations in which whatever is done is excellent.

26

These are the ten qualities of genuine Dharma:

The arising in the world of the ten virtues, the six perfections, all emptinesses, the factors of awakening, the four noble truths, the four *dhyanas*, the four formless absorptions, the ripening and liberating aspects of mantra, and so forth, is a quality of genuine Dharma.

The arising in the world of august lineages of human monarchs, august lineages of brahmins, august lineages of householders, the six types of gods of the desire realm (such as the four great kings), the seventeen types of gods of the form realm, and the four types of formless gods, are qualities of genuine Dharma.

The presence and arising in the world of stream-enterers, once-returners, non-returners, arhats, *pratyekabuddhas*, and utterly omniscient buddhas, is a quality of genuine Dharma. [32]

The arising of spontaneous benefit of sentient beings by the two form bodies—self-arisen compassion—until samsara is emptied, due to the power of bodhicitta and aspirations, is a quality of genuine Dharma.

Since all excellent means of sustaining sentient beings appropriately arise through the power of the aspirations of bodhisattvas, these are qualities of genuine Dharma.

Since the slight, brief happiness that is experienced in lower migrations and unrestful states is due to the merit of virtuous actions, this is a quality of genuine Dharma. [33]

When a bad person's mind turns to genuine Dharma and he or she becomes a holy person, respected by everyone, this is a quality of genuine Dharma.

When someone who, by carelessly engaging in wrongdoing has amassed the causes to become fuel for the fires of hell, turns his or her mind to genuine Dharma and achieves the happiness of higher states and liberation, this is a quality of genuine Dharma.

The delight and respect that all feel for someone who merely has faith in genuine Dharma, or interest in it, or liking for it, or merely retains the costume of it, is a quality of genuine Dharma.

The arising of abundant means of sustenance for those who abandon all possessions and, leaving home, become homeless and hide away in isolated hermitages, is a quality of genuine Dharma.

Those are ten summaries of the qualities of genuine Dharma. [34]

27

These are the ten things that are merely names:
Since the nature of the ground is indescribable, *ground* is merely a name.
Since in the path there is nothing to be traversed and no one traversing it, *path* is merely a name.
Since in the way things are there is nothing to be viewed and no viewer, *realization* is merely a name.
Since in the natural state there is nothing to meditate upon and no meditator, *experience* is merely a name.
Since in the ultimate nature there is nothing to be done and no doer, *conduct* is merely a name.
Since ultimately there is nothing to be guarded and no guard, *samaya* is merely a name.
Since ultimately there is nothing to be accumulated and no accumulator, *the two accumulations* is merely a name.
Since ultimately there is nothing to be purified and no purifier, *the two obscurations* is merely a name.
Since ultimately there is nothing to be abandoned and no abandoner, *samsara* is merely a name.
Since ultimately there is nothing to be attained and no attainer, *fruition* is merely a name.
Those are the ten things that are merely names.

28

These are the ten things that are spontaneously present as great bliss:
Since the nature of the minds of all sentient beings is the *dharmakaya*, it is spontaneously present as great bliss.
Since in the ground, the expanse of dharmata, there are no elaborations of characteristics, it is spontaneously present as great bliss. [35]

Since in realization that transcends the intellect and is beyond extremes there are no elaborations of division, it is spontaneously present as great bliss.
Since in experience free from mental activity there are no conceptual elaborations, it is spontaneously present as great bliss.
Since in effortless conduct free from action there are no elaborations of acceptance and rejection, it is spontaneously present as great bliss.
Since in the dharmakaya—indivisible space and wisdom—there are no elaborations of the apprehended and the apprehending, it is spontaneously present as great bliss.
Since in the sambhogakaya—self-arisen compassion—there are no elaborations of birth, death, transference, or change, it is spontaneously present as great bliss.
Since in the nirmanakaya—self-arising compassion—there are no elaborations of the perception of dualistic appearances, it is spontaneously present as great bliss.
Since in the *dharmachakra* of the doctrine there are no elaborations of the view of a self or of characteristics, it is spontaneously present as great bliss.
Since in the activity of boundless compassion there is no partiality or season, it is spontaneously present as great bliss. [36]
Those are the ten things that are spontaneously present as great bliss.

That completes *A Precious Garland of the Supreme Path,* a collection of the stainless instructions heard from the kind Kadampa gurus of the tradition of the glorious Dipankara [Atisha], father and son [Dromtonpa], acclaimed as the illuminators of the doctrine in the northern Himalayan region by gurus endowed with undefiled wisdom and by yidams such as Jetsun Drolma; and from the king of Jetsuns, Milarepa, the holder of the heart-nectar of learned siddhas such as Marpa of Lhodrak and the supreme beings Naro and Maitri, as renowned in India as the sun and moon. This was written by Sonam Rinchen, the meditator of Nyi, from Dakpo in the East, a holder of the treasury of the Kadampa and mahamudra instructions. [37]

[Colophon:]

In the words of Lord Gampopa: "To all future individuals devoted to me who think they cannot meet me: Please read the treatises composed by me, such as *A Precious Garland of the Supreme Path* and *The Ornament of Precious Liberation*. It will be no different from meeting me personally." Since he has said this, you fortunate ones devoted to Lord Gampopa, please be diligent in the propagation of these texts.

[Dedication by the sponsor of the woodblocks, Tsering Döndrup:]

The great sun of the Victor's teachings,
Dzamling Drakpa, out of compassion for beings,
Composed this Precious Garland of the Supreme Path.
In order to serve the teachings in this life,
In order that, in the long run, all our kind parents, who fill space,
May accomplish the two aims and attain true buddhahood,
And to spread the Victor's teachings in all directions through explanation and practice,
This wood block was newly produced at Karmapa's Dharma settlement,
Where it remains. May it become a beacon for devotees.
Sarva mangalam.

The Tibetan Text

༄༅།། [1] །རྗེ་སྒམ་པོ་པའི་ཞལ་གདམས། ལམ་མཆོག་རིན་པོ་ཆེའི་ཕྲེང་
བ་བཞུགས་སོ། ། [2] ༄༅།། །ན་མོ་རཏྣ་གུ་རུ། གང་ཞིག་འཁོར་བའི་རྒྱ་
མཚོ་འཇིགས་སུ་རུང་ཞིང་བརྒལ་དཀའ་བ་ལས་སྒྲོལ་བར་མཛད་པའི་བཀའ་
བརྒྱུད་རིན་པོ་ཆེའི་སྤྱོད་པ་རྣམ་པར་དག་པས་བརྒྱན་ཞིང་། །བྱིན་རླབས་ཀྱི་ཆུ་
རྒྱུན་རྒྱ་མཚོ་ཆེན་པོའི་དབྱིངས་ལྟར་ཟད་མི་ཤེས་པ། སྨོན་ལམ་རྒྱ་ཆེ་ཞིང་ཡུན་
རིང་བ་ལྷུན་གྱི་གྲུབ་པའི་སྒྲུབ་བརྒྱུད་དྲི་མ་མེད་པའི་བླ་མ་དམ་པ་རྣམས་ལ་ཕྱག་
འཚལ་ཞིང་སྐྱབས་སུ་མཆིའོ། །བྱིན་གྱིས་བརླབ་ཏུ་གསོལ་ལོ། །བཀའ་བརྒྱུད་
དེ་དག་ལས་ [3] །བྱུང་བའི་གསུང་གི་རྒྱུན་ཡུན་རིང་པོར་ཡིད་ལ་བརྟག་པར་
བྱས་ཏེ། །དངོས་དང་བརྒྱུད་ཀྱིས་རང་ཉིད་ལ་ཡིད་གདུང་བའི་སྐལ་ལྡན་རྣམས་
ལ་ཤིན་ཏུ་གཅེས་པའི་གདམས་ངག །ལམ་མཆོག་ཏུ་གྱུར་པའི་རིན་པོ་ཆེའི་
ཕྲེང་བ་ཞིག་ཡི་གེའི་རིས་སུ་བཀོད་པར་བགྱིའོ། །དེ་ཡང་རྟེན་གྱི་གང་ཟག་ཐར་
པ་དང་ཐམས་ཅད་མཁྱེན་པའི་སངས་རྒྱས་ཐོབ་པར་འདོད་པས། །དང་པོར་

ཡོངས་པའི་ཆོས་བཅུ་རྗེས་སུ་དྲན་པར་བྱ་བ་ནི། །རྙེད་པར་དཀའ་བའི་མི་ལུས་གཙང་ [4] མ་འདི། མི་དགེ་སྡིག་པའི་ལས་ལ་སྤྱོད་དུ་ཡོངས། །ལྡན་པར་དཀའ་བའི་དལ་འབྱོར་མི་ལུས་གཙང་མ་འདི། །ཆོས་མེད་ཐ་མལ་གྱི་ལུས་སུ་ཤི་རུ་ཡོངས། །སྙིགས་མའི་དུས་ཀྱི་མི་ཚེ་ཡུན་ཐུང་ཡུད་ཙམ་འདི། །དོན་མེད་བྱ་བའི་ལས་ལ་ཟད་དུ་ཡོངས། །རང་སེམས་ཆོས་སྐུའི་རང་བཞིན་སྤྲོས་མེད་འདི། །འཁྲུལ་པ་འཁོར་བའི་འདམ་དུ་བྱིང་དུ་ཡོངས། །ལམ་སྟོན་འདྲེན་པའི་བླ་མ་དམ་པ་དེ། །བྱང་ཆུབ་མ་ཐོབ་བར་དུ་འབྲལ་དུ་ཡོངས། །ཐར་པའི་གྲུ་གཟིངས་སྡོམ་པ་དམ་ཚིག་སྟེ། །ཉོན་མོངས་བག་མེད་རྐྱེན་དབང་གིས་བཤིག་ཏུ་ཡོངས། །བླ་མའི་རྐྱེན་གྱིས་རང་ལས་རྙེད་པའི་ཉམས་རྟོགས་དེ། །འདུ་བྱེད་ཚང་ཚིང་གི་གསེབ་ཏུ་སྟོང་དུ་ཡོངས། །གྲུབ་ཐོབ་རྣམས་ཀྱི་མན་ངག་ཟབ་མོ་སྟེ། །མི་ནག་སྐལ་མེད་རྣམས་ལ་ཟོང་དུ་བཙོང་དུ་ཡོངས། །འགྲོ་བ་སེམས་ཅན་དྲིན་ཅན་ཕ་མ་རྣམས། །སྡང་བའི་སེམས་ཀྱིས་སྤྱོང་ཞིང་འདོར་བ་ཡོངས། །གཞོན་པའི་ལང་ཚོ་དར་བའི་སྒོ་གསུམ་སྟེ། །ཐ་མལ་བཏང་སྙོམས [5] །ངང་དུ་བཞག་ཏུ་ཡོངས། །དེ་ནི་ཡོངས་པའི་ཆོས་བཅུ་ཡིན་ནོ། །དགོས་པའི་ཆོས་བཅུ་ནི། རང་གི་ཕོ་ཆོད་ཟིན་པས་གྲོས་ཀྱི་གཞི་རྩ་མ་འཆུགས་པ་ཞིག་དགོས། །དད་པ་དང་བརྩོན་འགྲུས་ཀྱིས་བླ་མ་དམ་པའི་བཀའ་བཞིན་སྒྲུབ་པ་ཞིག་དགོས། །གདམས་ངག་གི་སྐྱོན་ཡོན་ཤེས་པས་བླ་མའི་གདམས་ངག་འདོམ་ཁ་མ་ནོར་བ་ཞིག་དགོས། །ཤེས་རབ་དང་དད་པ་ནན་ཏན་གྱིས་བླ་མ་དམ་པའི་ཐུགས་དགོངས་ལོན་པ་ཞིག་དགོས། །དྲན་པ་དང་ཤེས་བཞིན་བག་ཡོད་དང་ལྡན་པས་སྒོ་གསུམ་ཉེས་སྐྱོན་

གྱིས་མ་གོས་པ་ཞིག་དགོས། །གོ་ཆ་དང་སྙིང་སྟོབས་ཀྱིས་ཡི་དམ་བརྟན་ཞིང་ཚུགས་ཐུབ་པ་ཞིག་དགོས། །ཆགས་མེད་ཞེན་མེད་ཀྱི་སྤྱོད་པས་སྣ་ཐག་མི་ལ་མ་ཤོར་བ་ཞིག་དགོས། །སྦྱོར་དངོས་རྗེས་གསུམ་གྱིས་ཟིན་པས་རྟག་ཏུ་ཚོགས་གཉིས་གསོག་པ་ལ་བརྩོན་པ་ཞིག་དགོས། །བྱམས་པ་དང་སྙིང་རྗེས་དངོས་སམ་བརྒྱུད་ནས་སེམས་ཅན་གྱི་དོན་ལ་བློ་ཕྱོགས་ [6] པ་ཞིག་དགོས། །ཤེས་རབ་དང་གོ་རྟོགས་ཀྱིས་ཆོས་ཐམས་ཅད་དངོས་པོ་དང་མཚན་མར་མ་ཤོར་བ་ཞིག་དགོས། །དེ་ནི་དགོས་པའི་ཆོས་བཅུ་ཡིན་ནོ། །བསྟེན་པར་བྱ་བའི་ཆོས་བཅུ་ནི། །རྟོགས་པ་དང་ཐུགས་རྗེ་ར་ལྡན་པའི་བླ་མ་དམ་པ་བསྟེན། །དབེན་ཞིང་ཉམས་དགའ་ལ་བྱིན་ཆགས་པའི་དགོན་པ་བསྟེན། །ལྟ་སྤྱོད་མཐུན་ཞིང་བློ་ཐུབ་པའི་གྲོགས་པོ་བསྟེན། །འཚོ་བའི་ཡོ་བྱད་ཀྱི་སྐྱོན་དྲན་ཞིང་ཚོད་ཟིན་པ་བསྟེན། །གྲུབ་ཐོབ་བརྒྱུད་པའི་མན་ངག་ཕྱོགས་མེད་བསྟེན། །རང་གཞན་ལ་ཕན་པའི་རྫས་སྨན་སྔགས་དང་རྟེན་འབྲེལ་ཟབ་མོ་བསྟེན། །ཁམས་དང་འཕྲོད་པའི་ཟས་དང་ཐབས་ལམ་བསྟེན། །ཉམས་ལ་ཕན་པའི་ཆོས་དང་སྤྱོད་ལམ་བསྟེན། །དད་གུས་སྐལ་པར་ལྡན་པའི་སློབ་མ་བསྟེན། །སྤྱོད་ལམ་རྣམ་བཞིར་རྒྱུན་དུ་དྲན་པ་དང་ཤེས་བཞིན་བསྟེན། །དེ་ནི་བསྟེན་པར་བྱ་བའི་ཆོས་བཅུའོ། །སྤང་བར་བྱ་བའི་ཆོས་བཅུ་ནི། །ཅི་བྱེད་འཇིག་རྟེན་ཆོས་བརྒྱད་དང་འདྲེས་པའི་སློབ་ [7] །དཔོན་སྤང་། །སེམས་དང་ཉམས་ལ་གནོད་པའི་འཁོར་འདབ་དང་གྲོགས་ངན་སྤང་། །གཡེང་བ་ཆེ་ཞིང་འཚེ་བ་མང་བའི་གནས་དང་དགོན་པ་སྤང་། །རྐུ་འཕྲོག་གཡོ་སྒྱུས་བསྒྲུབས་པའི་འཚོ་བ་སྤང་། །སེམས་དང་ཉམས་ལ་གནོད་པའི་ལས་དང་བྱ་བ་སྤང་།

།ཁམས་ལ་གནོད་པའི་ཟས་དང་སྤྱོད་ལམ་སྤང་། །འདོད་འདུན་སེར་སྣས་བཅིངས་པའི་འཛིན་ཆགས་སྤང་། །ཕ་རོལ་མི་དད་པའི་རྒྱུ་བག་མེད་པའི་སྤྱོད་ལམ་སྤང་། དོན་མེད་འགྲོ་འདུག་གི་ལས་དང་བྱ་བ་སྤང་། །རང་སྐྱོན་སྦས་ནས་གཞན་སྐྱོན་སྒྲོག་པ་སྤང་། །དེ་ནི་སྤང་བར་བྱ་བའི་ཆོས་བཅུའོ། །མི་སྤང་བར་བྱ་བའི་ཆོས་བཅུ་ནི། །སྙིང་རྗེ་གཞན་དོན་གྱི་རྩ་བ་ཡིན་པས་མི་སྤང་། །སྣང་བ་སེམས་ཀྱི་རང་འོད་ཡིན་པས་མི་སྤང་། །རྣམ་རྟོག་ཆོས་ཉིད་ཀྱི་རོལ་པ་ཡིན་པས་མི་སྤང་། །ཉོན་མོངས་ཡེ་ཤེས་ཀྱི་གསལ་འདེབས་ཡིན་པས་མི་སྤང་། །འདོད་ཡོན་ཉམས་རྟོགས་ཀྱི་ཆུ་ལུད་ཡིན་པས་མི་སྤང་། [8] ན་ཚ་སྡུག་བསྔལ་དགེ་བའི་བཤེས་གཉེན་ཡིན་པས་མི་སྤང་། །དགྲ་བགེགས་ཆོས་ཉིད་ཀྱི་བསྐུལ་མ་ཡིན་པས་མི་སྤང་། །ཤུགས་ལ་བྱུང་ན་དངོས་གྲུབ་ཡིན་པས་མི་སྤང་། །ཐབས་ལམ་གང་ཡང་ཤེས་རབ་ཀྱི་ལམ་སྐེགས་ཡིན་པས་མི་སྤང་། །གྲུབ་ཅིང་ལྡོགས་པའི་ལུས་ཀྱི་ཆོས་སྤྱོད་མི་སྤང་། །ནུས་པ་ཆུང་ཡང་གཞན་དོན་གྱི་བསམ་པ་མི་སྤང་། །དེ་ནི་མི་སྤང་བར་བྱ་བའི་ཆོས་བཅུ་ཡིན་ནོ། །ཤེས་པར་བྱ་བའི་ཆོས་བཅུ་ནི། །ཕྱིའི་སྣང་བ་འཁྲུལ་པར་འདུག་པས་བདེན་མེད་དུ་ཤེས་པར་བྱ། །ནང་གི་སེམས་ཉིད་བདག་མེད་དུ་འདུག་པས་སྟོང་པར་ཤེས་པར་བྱ། །བར་གྱི་རྣམ་རྟོག་རྐྱེན་སྐྱེས་སུ་འདུག་པས་གློ་བུར་དུ་ཤེས་པར་བྱ། །འབྱུང་བའི་ལུས་ངག་འདུས་བྱས་སུ་འདུག་པས་མི་རྟག་པར་ཤེས་པར་བྱ། །སེམས་ཅན་གྱི་བདེ་སྡུག་ཐམས་ཅད་ལས་ལས་འབྱུང་བས་ལས་འབྲས་མི་བསླུ་བར་ཤེས་པར་བྱ། །སྡུག་བསྔལ་ངེས་འབྱུང་གི་རྒྱུ་རུ་འདུག་པས་དགེ་བའི་བཤེས་གཉེན་དུ་ [9] ཤེས་པར་བྱ། །བདེ་སྐྱིད་འཁོར་

བའི་རྩ་བར་འདུག་པས་ཞེན་ཆགས་བདུད་དུ་ཤེས་པར་བྱ། །འདུ་འཛི་ཆོས་
ཀྱི་འགལ་རྐྱེན་དུ་འདུག་པས་བསོད་ནམས་བར་ཆད་དུ་ཤེས་པར་བྱ། །བར་
ཆད་དགེ་སྦྱོང་གི་བསྐུལ་མར་འདུག་པས་དགྲ་བགེགས་བླ་མར་ཤེས་པར་བྱ། །དོན་
དམ་པར་ཆོས་ཐམས་ཅད་རང་བཞིན་མེད་པར་འདུག་པས་གང་ལ་ཡང་མཉམ་
པ་ཉིད་དུ་ཤེས་པར་བྱ། །དེ་ནི་ཤེས་པར་བྱ་བའི་ཆོས་བཅུ་ཡིན་ནོ། །ཉམས་
སུ་བླང་བའི་ཆོས་བཅུ་ནི། །ཆོས་སྒོར་ཞུགས་ནས་མི་ཆོས་ཀྱི་ཁྲུ་རུ་མི་འཇུག་
པར་ཆོས་བཞིན་ཉམས་སུ་བླང་། །ཕ་ཡུལ་སྤངས་ནས་མི་ཡུལ་དུ་གཞི་མི་འདིང་
བར་ཆགས་མེད་དུ་ཉམས་སུ་བླང་། །བླ་མ་དམ་པ་བསྟེན་ནས་ང་རྒྱལ་སྤངས་
ཏེ་བཀའ་བཞིན་ཉམས་སུ་བླང་། །ཐོས་བསམ་ལ་བློ་སྦྱངས་ནས་ཁ་བཤད་མི་
བྱ་བར་ཤེས་པ་དོན་ཐོག་ཏུ་ཉམས་སུ་བླང་། །རྟོགས་པ་རྒྱུད་ལ་ཤར་ནས་ཕྱལ་
པར་བཏང་སྙོམས་སུ་མི་བཏང་བར་ཡེངས་མེད་དུ་ཉམས་སུ་བླང་། །ཉམས་ [10]
ལེན་རྒྱུད་ལ་སྐྱེས་ནས་ཚོགས་སུ་འདུ་འཛི་ལ་མི་འཇུག་པར་ཉམས་སུ་བླང་། །ཁས་
བླངས་ཤིང་དམ་བཅས་ནས་སྒོ་གསུམ་བག་མེད་ལ་མི་བཏང་བར་བསླབ་པ་གསུམ་
ཉམས་སུ་བླང་། །བྱང་ཆུབ་མཆོག་ཏུ་སེམས་བསྐྱེད་ནས་རང་དོན་མི་བྱེད་པར་
ཅི་བྱེད་གཞན་དོན་དུ་ཉམས་སུ་བླང་། །སྔགས་ཀྱི་སྒོར་ཞུགས་ནས་སྒོ་གསུམ་ཐ་
མལ་དུ་མི་བཞག་པར་དཀྱིལ་འཁོར་གསུམ་དུ་ཉམས་སུ་བླང་། །གཞོན་པའི་དུས་
སུ་དོན་མེད་ས་མཐའ་མི་བསྐོར་བ་བཤེས་གཉེན་དམ་པའི་ཞབས་དྲུང་དུ་དཀའ་
ཐུབ་ཉམས་སུ་བླང་ངོ་། །དེ་ནི་ཉམས་སུ་བླང་བའི་ཆོས་བཅུ་ཡིན་ནོ། །ནན་ཏན་
དུ་བྱ་བའི་ཆོས་བཅུ་ནི། །ལས་དང་པོ་པས་ཐོས་བསམ་ལ་ནན་ཏན་བྱ། །ཉམས་

སྒོང་སྐྱེས་ནས་སྒོམ་བསྒྲུབ་ལ་ནན་ཏན་བྱ། །བརྟན་པ་མ་ཐོབ་བར་དབེན་པ་ལ་ནན་ཏན་བྱ། །འཕྲོ་གོད་ཤས་ཆེ་ན་རིག་པ་གཏུན་པ་ལ་ནན་ཏན་བྱ། །བྱིང་རྨུག་ཤས་ཆེ་ན་རིག་པ་གཡེར་བ་ལ་ནན་ཏན་བྱ། །བློ་མ་བརྟན་བར་དུ་མཉམ་བཞག་ལ་ནན་ཏན་བྱ། །མཉམ་བཞག་ལ་བརྟེན་ནས་ [11] རྗེས་ཐོབ་ལ་ནན་ཏན་བྱ། །མི་མཐུན་པའི་འགལ་རྐྱེན་མང་ན་བཟོད་པ་གསུམ་ལ་ནན་ཏན་བྱ། །འདོད་འདུན་ཆགས་ཞེན་ཆེ་ན་ཞེན་པ་བཙན་ཐབས་སུ་ལོག་པ་ལ་ནན་ཏན་བྱ། བྱམས་དང་སྙིང་རྗེ་ཤས་ཆུང་ན་བྱང་ཆུབ་ཀྱི་སེམས་སྦྱོང་བ་ལ་ནན་ཏན་བྱ། །དེ་ནི་ནན་ཏན་བྱ་བའི་ཆོས་བཅུའོ། །བསྐུལ་མ་གདབ་པའི་ཆོས་བཅུ་ནི། །དལ་འབྱོར་རྙེད་དཀའ་བ་ལ་བསམས་ཏེ་དམ་པའི་ཆོས་ལ་བསྐུལ་མ་གདབ། །འཆི་བ་མི་རྟག་པ་ལ་བསམས་ཏེ་དགེ་སྦྱོར་ལ་བསྐུལ་མ་གདབ། །ལས་རྒྱུ་འབྲས་མི་བསླུ་བ་ལ་བསམས་ཏེ་སྡིག་པ་མི་དགེ་བ་སྤང་བ་ལ་བསྐུལ་མ་གདབ། །འཁོར་བའི་ཉེས་དམིགས་ལ་བསམས་ཏེ་ཐར་པ་སྒྲུབ་པ་ལ་བསྐུལ་མ་གདབ། །འཁོར་བའི་སེམས་ཅན་གྱི་སྡུག་བསྔལ་ལ་བསམས་ཏེ་བྱང་ཆུབ་ཀྱི་སེམས་སྦྱང་བ་ལ་བསྐུལ་མ་གདབ། །སེམས་ཅན་གྱི་བློ་ཕྱིན་ཅི་ལོག་ཏུ་འཁྲུལ་པ་ལ་བསམས་ཏེ་ཐོས་བསམ་ལ་བསྐུལ་མ་གདབ། །འཁྲུལ་པའི་བག་ཆགས་སྤངས་བར་དཀའ་བ་ལ་བསམས་ཏེ་སྒོམ་ [12] བསྒྲུབ་ལ་བསྐུལ་མ་གདབ། །སྙིགས་མའི་དུས་འདིར་ཉོན་མོངས་པ་བསྡོ་བ་ལ་བསམས་ཏེ་གཉེན་པོ་ལ་བསྐུལ་མ་གདབ། །སྙིགས་མའི་དུས་འདིར་འགལ་རྐྱེན་མང་བ་ལ་བསམས་ཏེ་བཟོད་པ་ལ་བསྐུལ་མ་གདབ། །ཕར་ཡེངས་ཚུར་ཡེངས་ཡེངས་མ་ལམ་ལ་མི་ཚེ་སྟོང་ཟད་དུ་སོང་བ་ལ་བསམས

ཏེ་བརྟོན་འགྲུས་ལ་བསྐུལ་མ་གདབ། །དེ་ནི་བསྐུལ་མ་གདབ་པའི་ཆོས་བཅུ་ཡིན་ནོ། །འཆོར་ས་བཅུ་ནི། །དད་པ་ཆུང་ལ་ཤེས་རབ་ཆེ་ན་ཁ་བཤད་མཁན་དུ་འཆོར་བ་ཡིན། དད་པ་ཆེ་ལ་ཤེས་རབ་ཆུང་ན་ཕྱུག་བཙིར་ཨ་འཐས་སུ་འཆོར་བ་ཡིན། །སྙིང་རུས་ཆེ་ལ་གདམས་ངག་མེད་ན་སྐྱོན་དང་གོལ་སར་འཆོར་བ་ཡིན། །སྔོན་དུ་ཐོས་བསམ་གྱི་སྒྲོ་འདོགས་མ་དཔྱད་ན་སྒོམ་ལུན་པའི་སྐྱེ་མཆེད་དུ་འཆོར་བ་ཡིན། །གོ་རྟོགས་སོ་མ་ལ་ཉམས་ལེན་མ་བྱས་ན་དྲེད་པོ་ཆོས་རྒྱུས་མཁན་དུ་འཆོར་བ་ཡིན། །ཐབས་སྙིང་རྗེ་ཆེན་པོ་ལ་བློ་མ་སྦྱངས་ན་ལམ་ཐེག་པ་དམན་པར་འཆོར་བ་ཡིན། །ཤེས་རབ་སྟོང་པ་ཉིད་ལ་བློ་མ་སྦྱངས་ན་ཅི་བྱས་འཁོར་བའི་ [13] ལམ་དུ་འཆོར་བ་ཡིན། །འཇིག་རྟེན་ཆོས་བརྒྱད་ཀྱི་མགོ་མ་སྙོམས་ན་ཅི་བྱེད་འཇིག་རྟེན་གྱི་རྒྱན་དུ་འཆོར་བ་ཡིན། །གྲོང་པའི་སྐྱེ་བོ་ཡི་དད་འདུན་མང་ན་མི་ནག་གི་ངོ་བསྲུང་དུ་འཆོར་བ་ཡིན། །ཡོན་ཏན་དང་ནུས་མཐུ་ཆེ་ལ་བློ་མི་བརྟན་ན་མི་ནག་གི་གྲོང་ཆོག་མཁན་དུ་འཆོར་བ་ཡིན། །དེ་ནི་འཆོར་ས་བཅུ་ཡིན་ནོ། །འདྲ་མིན་གྱི་ནོར་ས་བཅུ་ནི། །དད་པ་དང་འདོད་པ་ལ་ནོར་ས་ཡོད། །བྱམས་སྙིང་རྗེ་དང་ཆགས་པ་ལ་ནོར་ས་ཡོད། །ཤེས་བྱ་གཤིས་ཀྱི་སྟོང་པ་དང་བློས་བྱས་ཀྱི་སྟོང་པ་ལ་ནོར་ས་ཡོད། །ཆོས་ཀྱི་དབྱིངས་དང་ཆད་ལྟ་ལ་ནོར་ས་ཡོད། །ཉམས་མྱོང་དང་རྟོགས་པ་ལ་ནོར་ས་ཡོད། །བཙུན་པོ་དང་རྒྱལ་འཆོས་ལ་ནོར་ས་ཡོད། །འཕྲུལ་ཞིག་དང་བདུད་ཁྲིར་ལ་ནོར་ས་ཡོད། །གྲུབ་ཐོབ་དང་ཟོག་པོ་ལ་ནོར་ས་ཡོད། །གཞན་དོན་བྱེད་པ་དང་རང་དོན་བྱེད་པ་ལ་ནོར་ས་ཡོད། །ཐབས་མཁས་པ་དང་གཡོ་སྒྱུ་ལ་ནོར་ས་ཡོད། །དེ་

ནི་འདྲ་མིན་གྱི་ནོར་ས་བཅུའོ། །མ་ནོར་བའི་ཆོས་བཅུ་ནི། །དངོས་པོ་གང་ལ་ཡང་མ་ཆགས་པར་ཁྱིམ་ནས་ཁྱིམ་ [14] མེད་པར་རབ་ཏུ་བྱུང་བ་ནི་མ་ནོར་བ་ཡིན། །བླ་མ་དམ་པ་དགེ་བའི་བཤེས་གཉེན་མགོ་ལ་ཐོད་བཞིན་དུ་ཁུར་བ་ནི་མ་ནོར་བ་ཡིན། །ཆོས་ལ་ཐོས་བསམ་བསྒོམ་གསུམ་ཟླུག་མར་བྱེད་པ་རྣམས་ནི་མ་ནོར་བ་ཡིན། །ལྟ་བ་མཐོ་ལ་སྤྱོད་པ་དམའ་བ་ནི་མ་ནོར་བ་ཡིན། །བློ་ཡངས་ལ་དམ་བཅའ་དོག་པ་ནི་མ་ནོར་བ་ཡིན། །ཤེས་རབ་ཆེ་ལ་ང་རྒྱལ་ཆུང་བ་ནི་མ་ནོར་བ་ཡིན། །གདམས་ངག་ཕྱུག་ལ་ཉམས་ལེན་ལ་བརྩོན་པ་ནི་མ་ནོར་བ་ཡིན། །ཉམས་རྟོགས་བཟང་ལ་ང་རྒྱལ་ཧློམ་སེམས་མེད་པ་ནི་མ་ནོར་བ་ཡིན། །གཅིག་པུར་སྡོད་ཚུགས་ལ་ཚོགས་སུ་ཡན་ཐུབ་པ་ནི་མ་ནོར་བ་ཡིན། །རང་དོན་འཁྲིས་མེད་པ་ལ་གཞན་དོན་གྱི་ཐབས་ལ་མཁས་པ་ནི་མ་ནོར་བ་ཡིན། །དེ་ནི་མ་ནོར་བའི་ཆོས་བཅུ་ཡིན་ནོ། །དོན་མེད་པའི་ཆོས་བཅུ་བཞི་ནི། །མི་ལུས་ཐོབ་ནས་དམ་པའི་ཆོས་མི་དྲན་པ་ནི་རིན་པོ་ཆེའི་གླིང་དུ་ཕྱིན་ནས་སྟོང་ལོག་བྱས་པ་དང་འདྲ་སྟེ་དོན་མེད། །ཆོས་སྒོར་ཞུགས་ནས་ཁྱིམ་ཐབ་བྱེད་པ་ནི་ཕྱེ་མ་ལེབ་མར་མེ་ལ་འཕྱོང་བ་དང་འདྲ་སྟེ་དོན་མེད། །དད་མེད་ཆོས་མཛད་ཀྱི་ [15] དྲུང་ན་གནས་པ་ནི་རྒྱ་མཚོའི་འགྲམ་དུ་སྐོམ་གྱིར་ཤི་བ་དང་འདྲ་སྟེ་དོན་མེད། །རྩ་བ་བཞི་དང་བདག་ཏུ་འཛིན་པའི་གཉེན་པོར་མ་སོང་བའི་ཆོས་ནི། །སྤྲ་རེ་དང་སྡོང་པོ་ལྷན་ཅིག་ཏུ་བཞག་པ་དང་འདྲ་སྟེ་དོན་མེད། །ཉོན་མོངས་པའི་གཉེན་པོར་མ་སོང་བའི་མན་ངག་ནི། །ནད་པས་སྨན་ཁུལ་ཐོགས་པ་དང་འདྲ་སྟེ་དོན་མེད། །རྒྱུད་ཐོག་ཏུ་མ་ཁེལ་བའི་ཐ་སྙད་ལ་ལྕེ་སྦྱངས་པ་ནི། །ནེ་

ཅོའི་ཁ་ཏོན་བྱས་པ་དང་འདྲ་སྟེ་དོན་མེད། །ཀུ་འཕྲོག་གཡོ་སྒྱུས་མ་བྱིན་པར་བླངས་ནས་སྦྱིན་པ་བྱེད་པ་ནི། །སློག་པ་ཆུ་རུ་བཅུག་ནས་ཕྱུག་པ་དང་འདྲ་སྟེ་དོན་མེད། །སེམས་ཅན་ལ་གནོད་པ་བསྐྱལ་ནས་དཀོན་མཆོག་མཆོད་པ་ནི། །བུའི་ཤ་བཅད་ནས་མ་ལ་སྟེར་བ་དང་འདྲ་སྟེ་དོན་མེད། །ཚེ་འདིའི་རང་འདོད་ཀྱི་ཕྱིར་ཚུལ་འཆོས་དང་བཟོད་པ་དང་དུ་ལེན་པ་ནི། །བྱི་ལས་བྱི་བ་ལ་འཇབ་པ་དང་འདྲ་སྟེ་དོན་མེད། །ཚེ་འདིའི་སྙན་གྲགས་དང་རྙེད་བཀུར་འདོད་པས་དགེ་བ་རླབས་ཆེན་བྱེད་པ་ནི། །ཡིད་བཞིན་གྱི་ནོར་བུ་རིན་པོ་ཆེ་བེལ་བ་རྡོག་པོ་གཅིག་གམ་ [16] སྲང་ཟན་རྡོག་པོ་གཅིག་གམ། །ཟན་རྡོག་པོ་གཅིག་དང་བརྗེ་བ་དང་འདྲ་སྟེ་དོན་མེད། །མང་དུ་ཐོས་ཀྱང་རང་རྒྱུད་ཐ་མལ་དུ་ལུས་པ་ནི། །སྨན་པ་གཙོང་ནད་ཀྱིས་ཟིན་པ་དང་འདྲ་སྟེ་དོན་མེད། །གདམས་ངག་མཁས་ལ་ཉམས་མྱོང་མེད་པ་ནི། །ཕྱུག་པོའི་བང་མཛོད་ཀྱི་ལྡེ་མིག་མེད་པ་དང་འདྲ་སྟེ་དོན་མེད། །རང་གིས་ཆོས་ཀྱི་དོན་མ་རྟོགས་པར་གཞན་ལ་བཤད་པ་ནི། །ལོང་བས་ལོང་བ་ཁྲིད་པ་དང་འདྲ་སྟེ་དོན་མེད། །ཐབས་ལས་བྱུང་བའི་ཉམས་མྱོང་ལ་མཆོག་ཏུ་བཟུང་ནས་གནས་ལུགས་ཀྱི་དོན་མི་ཚོལ་བ་ནི། །ར་གན་ལ་གསེར་དུ་འཛིན་པ་དང་འདྲ་སྟེ་དོན་མེད། །དེ་ནི་དོན་མེད་པའི་ཆོས་བཅུ་བཞི་ཡིན་ནོ། །ཆོས་པའི་མཚང་བཅོ་བརྒྱད་ནི། །དབེན་པར་བསྡད་ནས་ཚེ་འདིའི་ཆེ་ཐབས་སྒྲུབ་པ་ནི་ཆོས་པའི་མཚང་། །ཚོགས་དཔོན་བྱས་ནས་རང་འདོད་སྒྲུབ་པ་ནི་ཆོས་པའི་མཚང་། །ཆོས་མཁས་པ་སྤྱོད་ལ་མི་འཇོམ་པ་ནི་ཆོས་པའི་མཚང་། །གདམས་ངག་ཆེ་ལ་རང་རྒྱུད་ཐ་མལ་དུ་ལུས་པ་ནི་ཆོས་པའི་མཚང་། །ཚུལ་ཁྲིམས་བསྲུན་

ལ་འདོད་པ་ཆེ་བ་ནི་ཆོས་ [17] །པའི་མཚང་། །ཉམས་རྟོགས་བཟང་ལ་
རང་རྒྱུད་མ་ཐུལ་བ་ནི་ཆོས་པའི་མཚང་། །ཆོས་སྒོར་ཞུགས་ནས་མི་ཆོས་ཀྱི་
ཆགས་སྡང་མ་སྤངས་པ་ནི་ཆོས་པའི་མཚང་། །མི་ཆོས་བཤོལ་དེ་ལྷ་ཆོས་བྱས་
ནས་སོ་ནམ་གྱི་བྱ་བ་མ་ཐེངས་པ་ནི་ཆོས་པའི་མཚང་། །དོན་གོ་བ་རྙེད་ནས་
ཉམས་སུ་མི་ལེན་པ་ནི་ཆོས་པའི་མཚང་། །ཉམས་ལེན་གྱི་དམ་བཅའ་བྱས་
ནས་སྡོད་མི་ཚུགས་པ་ནི་ཆོས་པའི་མཚང་། །བྱ་རྒྱུ་ཆོས་ལས་མེད་ཀྱང་སྤྱོད་
པ་སོ་མི་ཐུབ་པ་ནི་ཆོས་པའི་མཚང་། །ལྷོ་རྒྱབ་ཤུགས་ལས་འབྱུང་ཡང་སེམས་
ཆོལ་ཁྲོལ་ཞུགས་པ་ནི་ཆོས་པའི་མཚང་། །དགེ་སྦྱོར་གྱི་ནུས་པ་ནད་པ་དང་སྲིའུ་
ལ་སྤྱུགས་པ་ནི་ཆོས་པའི་མཚང་། །གདམས་ངག་ཟབ་མོ་ཟས་ནོར་གྱི་ཕྱིར་སྟོན་
པ་ནི་ཆོས་པའི་མཚང་། །བདག་ལ་ཐབས་ཀྱིས་བསྟོད་ཅིང་གཞན་ལ་ཐབས་ཀྱིས་
སྨོད་པ་ནི་ཆོས་པའི་མཚང་། །གདམས་ངག་གཞན་ལ་བཤད་ཅིང་རང་རྒྱུད་ཆོས་
དང་མི་མཐུན་པ་ནི་ཆོས་པའི་མཚང་། །གཅིག་པུར་སྡོད་མི་ཚུགས་ལ་མི་དང་
[18] འགྲོགས་མི་ཤེས་པ་ནི་ཆོས་པའི་མཚང་། །སྐྱིད་མི་ཐེག་ཅིང་སྡུག་མི་ཐུབ་
པ་ནི་ཆོས་པའི་མཚང་། །དེ་ནི་ཆོས་པའི་མཚང་བཅོ་བརྒྱད་དོ། །མེད་ཐབས་
མེད་པའི་ཆོས་བཅུ་གཉིས་ནི། །དང་པོ་སྐྱེ་ཤེས་གཏིང་ནས་འཇིགས་པའི་དད་
པ་བརྟན་པོ་ཅིག་མེད་ཐབས་མེད། །ཐར་པའི་ལམ་སྣ་འདྲེན་པའི་བླ་མ་ཅིག་
མེད་ཐབས་མེད། །རྒྱུད་ལ་དོན་གོ་བ་ལོངས་པའི་ཤེས་རབ་ཅིག་མེད་ཐབས་མེད།
།གོ་ཆ་དང་སྙིང་སྟོབས་སུ་ལྡན་པའི་བརྩོན་འགྲུས་ཅིག་མེད་ཐབས་མེད། །བསླབ་
གསུམ་དང་ཚོགས་གཉིས་ཀྱིས་ཚོག་པ་མེད་པའི་བསགས་པ་ཞིག་མེད་ཐབས་

མེད། །ཤེས་བྱའི་གནས་ལུགས་རྟོགས་པའི་ལྟ་བ་ཅིག་མེད་ཐབས་མེད། །སེམས་
ཉིད་གར་གཞག་ཏུ་གནས་པའི་སྒོམ་པ་ཞིག་མེད་ཐབས་མེད། །བྱེད་སྤྱོད་ཐམས་
ཅད་ལམ་དུ་ཁྱེར་བའི་སྤྱོད་པ་ཞིག་མེད་ཐབས་མེད། །རྒྱུན་བགེགས་བདུད་དང་
གོལ་ས་སྐྱོང་བའི་གདམས་ངག་ཆིག་ཏུ་མ་ལུས་པའི་ཉམས་ལེན་ཞིག་མེད་ཐབས་
མེད། །ལུས་སེམས་འབྲལ་ [19] །བའི་ཚེ་ན་བློ་བདེའི་ཞི་གདིང་ཆེན་པོ་
ཅིག་མེད་ཐབས་མེད། །སྐུ་གསུམ་རང་ལ་ལྷུན་གྱིས་གྲུབ་པའི་འབྲས་བུ་ཅིག་མེད་
ཐབས་མེད་དོ། །དེ་ནི་མེད་ཐབས་མེད་པའི་ཆོས་བཅུ་གཉིས་ཡིན་ནོ། །སྐྱེས་
བུ་དམ་པའི་རྟགས་བཅུ་གཅིག་ནི། །ཕྲག་དོག་དང་ང་རྒྱལ་ཆུང་བ་ནི་སྐྱེས་བུ་དམ་
པའི་རྟགས། །འདོད་པ་ཆུང་ཞིང་དངོས་པོ་ངན་ངོན་ཙམ་གྱིས་ཆོག་ཤེས་པ་ནི་
སྐྱེས་བུ་དམ་པའི་རྟགས། །སྒྲ་ཚུལ་དང་ཆེ་འགྱིང་དང་ང་རྒྱལ་མེད་པ་ནི་སྐྱེས་
བུ་དམ་པའི་རྟགས། །ཚུལ་འཆོས་དང་ངོ་ལྐོག་མེད་པ་ནི་སྐྱེས་བུ་དམ་པའི་རྟགས།
།བྱ་བ་གང་ཡང་བརྟགས་ཤིང་ཤེས་བཞིན་དུ་དཔྱད་ནས་ཤེས་བཞིན་དུ་དྲན་པས་
ཟིན་པར་བྱེད་པ་ནི་སྐྱེས་བུ་དམ་པའི་རྟགས། །ལས་རྒྱུ་འབྲས་མིག་གི་འབྲས་
བུ་བཞིན་བསྲུང་བ་ནི་སྐྱེས་བུ་དམ་པའི་རྟགས། །སྡོམ་པ་དང་དམ་ཚིག་ལ་ངོ་
ལྐོག་མེད་པ་ནི་སྐྱེས་བུ་དམ་པའི་རྟགས། །སེམས་ཅན་ལ་ཉེ་རིང་གསར་འགྲོགས་
མེད་པ་ནི་སྐྱེས་བུ་དམ་པའི་རྟགས། །གཞན་གྱིས་སྡིག་གསོག་པ་ལ་ཁོང་མི་ཁྲོ་
[20] ཞིང་བཟོད་པར་བྱེད་པ་ནི་སྐྱེས་བུ་དམ་པའི་རྟགས། །རྒྱལ་ཁ་ཐམས་ཅད་
མི་ལ་སྟེར་ཞིང་ཕམ་ཁ་རང་ལ་ལེན་པ་ནི་སྐྱེས་བུ་དམ་པའི་རྟགས། །བསམ་སྤྱོད་
གང་ལ་ཡང་འཇིག་རྟེན་པ་གཞན་དང་མི་མཐུན་པ་ནི་སྐྱེས་བུ་དམ་པའི་རྟགས།

།དེ་ནི་སྐྱེས་བུ་དམ་པའི་རྟགས་བཅུ་གཅིག་ཡིན་ནོ། །དེ་དག་ལས་ལོག་པ་ནི་སྐྱེས་བུ་དམ་པ་མིན་པའི་རྟགས་ཡིན་ནོ། །ཕན་པ་མེད་པའི་ཆོས་བཅུ་ནི། །སྒྱུ་མའི་ལུས་ལ་བསྙེན་བཀུར་དང་རིམ་གྲོ་ཇི་ཙམ་བྱས་ཀྱང་མི་རྟག་འཇིག་པར་ངེས་པའི་ཕན་པ་མེད། །ཟང་ཟིང་ནོར་ལ་སེར་སྣ་དང་བརྣབ་སེམས་ཅི་ཙམ་བྱས་ཀྱང་རང་འཆི་བའི་ནང་པར་སྒྲིན་མོ་ལག་སྟོང་དུ་འགྲོ་བས་ཕན་པ་མེད། །མཁར་པེའུ་དང་ཁང་བཟང་ལ་དཀའ་བ་ཇི་སྙེད་ཅིག་སྤྱད་ནས་བརྩིགས་ཀྱང་འཆི་བའི་ནང་པར་གཅིག་པུར་འགྲོ་ཞིང་རོ་ཡང་སྒོར་འདོན་པས་ཕན་པ་མེད། །བུ་དང་ཚ་བོ་ལ་བྱམས་པའི་སེམས་ཀྱིས་དངོས་པོ་ཇི་ཙམ་ཅིག་ཕོག་ཀྱང་འཆི་བའི་དུས་སུ་ཕན་སྟོབས་སྐད་ཅིག་ཀྱང་མེད་པས་ཕན་པ་མེད། །གཉེན་དང་གྲོགས་པོ་ལ་བརྩེ་གདུང་ [21] གི་སེམས་འཛིན་དང་ངོ་སྲུང་ཇི་སྙེད་ཅིག་བྱས་ཀྱང་རང་ཤི་བའི་ནང་པར་གཅིག་པུར་གྲོགས་མེད་དུ་འགྲོ་བས་ཕན་པ་མེད། །བུ་དང་ཚ་བོ་མང་ཡང་མི་རྟག་པས་བདག་གི་སྦྱིན་པའི་དངོས་པོ་བདོག་ཀྱང་འདོར་བར་ངེས་པས་ཕན་པ་མེད། །ཚེ་འདིའི་དོན་དུ་ས་སྤྱོད་མངའ་རིས་དང་ལས་ཐབས་ལ་འབད་རྩོལ་ཇི་སྙེད་ཅིག་བྱས་ཀྱང་རང་འཆི་བའི་ནང་པར་གནས་དང་འབྲེལ་པ་གཏན་མེད་དུ་འགྲོ་བས་ཕན་པ་མེད། །དད་པས་ཆོས་སྒོར་ཞུགས་ཀྱང་ཆོས་བཞིན་མ་སྤྱད་ན་ཆོས་ཀྱིས་སླར་ངན་སོང་དུ་འགྲོ་བའི་རྒྱུ་བྱེད་པས་ཕན་པ་མེད། །ཐོས་བསམ་ལ་བློ་སྦྱངས་ནས་ཆོས་ཇི་སྙེད་ཅིག་ཤེས་ཀྱང་ཉམས་སུ་མ་བླངས་ན་འཆི་ཁར་ལམ་དུ་ཁྱེར་རྒྱུ་མེད་པས་ཕན་པ་མེད། །དགེ་བའི་བཤེས་གཉེན་དམ་པའི་དྲུང་དུ་ཡུན་རིང་བསྡད་ཀྱང་རང་ལ་དད་གུས་མེད་ན་གོང་མའི་ཡོན་ཏན་དང་བྱིན་

ལྐབས་མི་འགོ་བས་ཕན་པ་མེད། །དེ་ནི་ཕན་པ་མེད་པའི་ཆོས་བཅུ་ཡིན་ནོ། །རང་སྡུག་རང་གིས་བྱས་པའི་ཆོས་བཅུ་ནི། །བཟའ་མེད་པའི་ཁྲིམ་ [22] ཐབ་བྱེད་པ་དེ་གླེན་པས་བཙན་དུག་ཟོས་པ་དང་འདྲ་སྟེ་རང་སྡུག་རང་གིས་ཉོས་པ་ཡིན། །ཆོས་མེད་སྡིག་པ་བྱེད་པ་དེ་སྨྱོན་པ་གཡང་ལ་འཕྱོང་བ་དང་འདྲ་སྟེ་རང་སྡུག་རང་གིས་བྱས་པ་ཡིན། །གཞན་ལ་ཟོལ་ཟོག་བྱེད་པ་དེ་དུག་ཅན་གྱི་ཁ་ཟས་འདྲེན་པ་དང་འདྲ་སྟེ་རང་སྡུག་རང་གིས་བྱས་པ་ཡིན། །ཀླད་ཆུང་མི་དཔོན་བྱེད་པ་དེ་རྒན་མོས་ཕྱུགས་སྐྱོང་བ་དང་འདྲ་སྟེ་རང་སྡུག་རང་གིས་བྱས་པ་ཡིན། །ལྷག་བསམ་གྱིས་གཞན་དོན་ལ་མི་བརྩོན་པར་ཆོས་བརྒྱད་ཀྱིས་རང་དོན་ལ་བརྩོན་པ་ནི་ལོང་བ་བྱང་ཐང་ལ་འཁོར་བ་དང་འདྲ་སྟེ་རང་སྡུག་རང་གིས་བྱས་པ་ཡིན། །མི་འགྲུབ་པའི་བྱ་བ་ཆེན་པོ་ཆེ་ལ་འཛུ་བ་ནི། །ཉམས་ཆུང་ཁུར་ཆེན་པོ་ཁུར་བ་དང་འདྲ་སྟེ་རང་སྡུག་རང་གིས་བྱས་པ་ཡིན། །ང་རྒྱལ་གྱིས་བླ་མ་དམ་པ་དང་རྒྱལ་བའི་བཀའ་ཁྲིད་དུ་གསོད་པ་དེ་དབང་པོ་ཆེའི་འདུན་མ་སྟོར་བ་དང་འདྲ་སྟེ་རང་སྡུག་རང་གིས་བྱས་པ་ཡིན། །ཉམས་ལེན་བཞོལ་ནས་མི་ནག་གི་གྲོང་ལ་འགྲིམ་པ་དེ་རི་དྭགས་ཀླུངས་སུ་བབས་པ་དང་འདྲ་སྟེ་རང་སྡུག་རང་གིས་ [23] །བྱས་པ་ཡིན། །གཉུག་མའི་ཡེ་ཤེས་མི་སྐྱོང་བར་འདུ་འཛིའི་སྤྲོས་པས་གཡེང་བར་བྱེད་པ་དེ་མཁའ་ལྡིང་གཤོག་པ་ཆག་པ་དང་འདྲ་སྟེ་རང་སྡུག་རང་གིས་བྱས་པ་ཡིན། །བླ་མ་དཀོན་མཆོག་གི་དཀོར་ལ་བག་མེད་དུ་སྤྱོད་པ་དེ་བུ་ཆུང་མི་མདག་འགམ་པ་དང་འདྲ་སྟེ་རང་སྡུག་རང་གིས་བྱས་པ་ཡིན། །དེ་ནི་རང་སྡུག་རང་གིས་བྱས་པའི་ཆོས་བཅུ་ཡིན་ནོ། །རང་དྲིན་རང་ལ་ཆེ་བའི་ཆོས་བཅུ་ནི། །མི་ཆོས་

ཀྱི་ཆགས་སྡང་སྤང་ནས་དམ་པའི་ལྷ་ཆོས་བྱེད་པ་ནི་རང་དྲིན་རང་ལ་ཆེ་བ་ཡིན། །ཁྲིམ་ཐབ་དང་གཉེན་གྲོགས་སྤངས་ནས་སྐྱེས་བུ་དམ་པ་བསྟེན་པ་དེ་རང་དྲིན་རང་ལ་ཆེ་བ་ཡིན། འདུ་འཛིའི་བྱ་བ་བཏང་ནས་ཐོས་བསམ་སྒོམ་གསུམ་བྱེད་པ་ནི་རང་དྲིན་རང་ལ་ཆེ་བ་ཡིན། །གྲོང་པ་དང་འདྲིས་བཤེས་སྤངས་ནས་གཅིག་པུར་དབེན་པར་སྡོད་པ་ནི་རང་དྲིན་རང་ལ་ཆེ་བ་ཡིན། །འདོད་ཡོན་གྱི་འཁྲི་བ་བཅད་ནས་ཆགས་མེད་ལ་ཆུགས་ཐུབ་པ་ནི་རང་དྲིན་རང་ལ་ཆེ་བ་ཡིན། །ངན་ངོན་ཙམ་ལ་ཆོག་ཤེས་ཤིང་བཟང་པོ་ལ་འདོད་འདུན་མེད་པ་ནི་རང་དྲིན་རང་ལ་ཆེ་བ་ཡིན། །རང་དབང་གཞན་ལ་མི་བསྒྱུར་བར་ཡི་དམ་ལ་བརྟན་པར་བྱེད་པ་ནི་རང་དྲིན་རང་ལ་ [24] །ཆེ་ བ་ཡིན། །ཚེ་འདི་ཡི་འཕྲུལ་བདེ་ལ་མི་བལྟ་བར་གཏན་དུ་བདེ་བའི་བྱང་ཆུབ་སྒྲུབ་པར་བྱེད་པ་ནི་རང་དྲིན་རང་ལ་ཆེ་བ་ཡིན། །དངོས་པོའི་མངོན་ཞེན་སྤངས་ནས་སྟོང་པ་ཉིད་ཉམས་སུ་ལེན་པ་ནི་རང་དྲིན་རང་ལ་ཆེ་བ་ཡིན། །སྒོ་གསུམ་ཐ་མལ་དུ་མི་སྡུད་པར་ཚོགས་གཉིས་ཟུང་དུ་འཇུག་པ་ལ་འབད་པ་ནི་རང་དྲིན་རང་ལ་ཆེ་བ་ཡིན། །དེ་ནི་རང་དྲིན་རང་ལ་ཆེ་བའི་ཆོས་བཅུ་ཡིན་ནོ། །ཡང་དག་པའི་ཆོས་བཅུ་ནི། ལས་རྒྱུ་འབྲས་ལ་ཡིད་ཆེས་པ་ནི་དབང་པོ་ཐ་མའི་ཡང་དག་པའི་ལྟ་བ་ཡིན། །ཕྱི་ནང་གི་ཆོས་ཐམས་ཅད་སྣང་བ་སྟོང་པ་རིག་པ་དང་སྟོང་པ་ཟུང་འཇུག་བཞིར་རྟོགས་པ་ནི་དབང་པོ་འབྲིང་གི་ཡང་དག་པའི་ལྟ་བ་ཡིན། །བལྟ་བྱ་ལྟ་བྱེད་རྟོགས་པ་གསུམ་དབྱེར་མེད་དུ་རྟོགས་པ་ནི་དབང་པོ་རབ་ཀྱི་ཡང་དག་པའི་ལྟ་བ་ཡིན། །དམིགས་པར་རྩེ་གཅིག་ལ་གནས་པ་ནི་དབང་པོ་ཐ་མའི་ཡང་དག་པའི་བསྒོམ་པ་ཡིན། །ཟུང་

འཇུག་བཞིའི་ཏིང་ངེ་འཛིན་ལ་གནས་པ་ནི་དབང་པོ་འབྲིང་གི་ཡང་དག་པའི་བསྒོམ་
པ་ཡིན། །བསྒོམ་བྱ་སྒོམ་བྱེད་ཉམས་ལེན་གསུམ་དབྱེར་མེད་ཅིང་མི་དམིགས་
[25] །པའི་ངང་ལ་གནས་པ་ནི་དབང་པོ་རབ་ཀྱི་ཡང་དག་པའི་བསྒོམ་པ་ཡིན།
།ལས་རྒྱུ་འབྲས་མིག་གི་འབྲས་བུ་བཞིན་སྲུང་བ་ནི་དབང་པོ་ཐ་མའི་ཡང་དག་པའི་
སྤྱོད་པ་ཡིན། །ཆོས་ཐམས་ཅད་རྨི་ལམ་སྒྱུ་མའི་ཚུལ་དུ་སྤྱོད་པ་ནི་དབང་པོ་
འབྲིང་གི་ཡང་དག་པའི་སྤྱོད་པ་ཡིན། །གང་ཅི་ལ་ཡང་མི་སྤྱོད་པ་ནི་དབང་པོ་རབ་
ཀྱི་ཡང་དག་པའི་སྤྱོད་པ་ཡིན། །བདག་འཛིན་དང་ཉོན་མོངས་པ་མཐའ་དག་ཇེ་
ཆུང་ཇེ་ཞི་ལ་སོང་བ་ནི་དབང་པོ་རབ་འབྲིང་ཐ་མ་གསུམ་ཀའི་ཡང་དག་པའི་དྲོད་
རྟགས་ཡིན་ནོ། །དེ་ནི་ཡང་དག་པའི་ཆོས་བཅུ་ཡིན་ནོ། །ཆོས་པའི་འཁྲུལ་པ་
བཅུ་ནི། །དམ་པའི་ཆོས་ཚུལ་བཞིན་སྒྲུབ་པའི་བླ་མ་ལ་མི་བསྟེན་པར་ཟོག་པོ་
ཁ་བཤད་མཁན་གྱི་རྗེས་སུ་འབྲང་བ་ནི་ཤིན་ཏུ་འཁྲུལ། །གྲུབ་ཐོབ་སྙན་རྒྱུད་ཀྱི་
གདམས་ངག་མི་ཚོལ་བར་དོན་མེད་ཀྱི་རིགས་པའི་ཆོས་ལ་ནན་ཏན་བྱེད་པ་ནི་
ཤིན་ཏུ་འཁྲུལ། །སྣང་བ་འཕྲལ་ཤར་ལ་མི་ཚེ་ཅི་ཕྱིད་མི་བྱེད་པར་གཏན་དུ་སྡོད་
ཆེས་ཀྱི་ཤོམ་ར་རྒྱུའི་ཆེ་བྱེད་པ་ནི་ཤིན་ཏུ་ [26] འཁྲུལ། །རང་གཅིག་པུར་
ཆོས་ཀྱི་དོན་ལ་མི་སེམས་པར་འཁོར་མང་གི་ནང་ན་ཆོས་བཤད་བྱེད་པ་ནི་ཤིན་
ཏུ་འཁྲུལ། །ལོངས་སྤྱོད་ཁ་ལྷག་མཆོད་སྦྱིན་དུ་མི་གཏོང་བར་སེར་སྣ་གཡོ་སྒྱུས་
ནོར་རྫས་གསོག་པ་ནི་ཤིན་ཏུ་འཁྲུལ། །དམ་ཚིག་སྡོམ་པ་ཚུལ་བཞིན་མི་བསྲུང་
བར་སྒོ་གསུམ་བག་མེད་འཆལ་པར་གཏོང་བ་ནི་ཤིན་ཏུ་འཁྲུལ། །གནས་ལུགས་
རྟོགས་པའི་དོན་ལ་གོམས་འདྲིས་མི་བྱེད་པར་མི་ཚེ་དོན་ཆུང་གི་བྱ་བྱེད་ཕར་

རེ་ཆུར་རེ་ལ་ཟད་པར་བྱེད་པ་ནི་ཤིན་ཏུ་འཁྲུལ། །འཁྲུལ་པ་ལང་ཙན་གྱི་རང་རྒྱུད་མི་ཐུལ་བར་དམུ་རྒོད་བྱེས་པའི་གཞན་རྒྱུད་འདུལ་བ་ཤིན་ཏུ་འཁྲུལ། །རྒྱུད་ལ་སྐྱེས་པའི་ཉམས་མྱོང་མི་སྐྱོང་བར་ཚེ་འདིའི་ཚེ་ཐབས་སྐྱོང་བ་ཤིན་ཏུ་འཁྲུལ། །ད་རེས་རྟེན་འབྲེལ་འཛོམ་པའི་ཐོག་ལ་བརྩོན་འགྲུས་མི་རྩོམ་པར་ལེ་ལོ་སྙོམས་ལས་ལ་དགའ་བ་ཤིན་ཏུ་འཁྲུལ། །དེ་ནི་ཆོས་པའི་འཁྲུལ་ས་བཅུ་ཡིན་ནོ། །དགོས་པའི་ཆོས་བཅུ་ནི། །དང་པོ་སྐྱེ་ཤིས་འཇིག་པའི་དད་པ་གཤའ་མ་ཤ་བ་བཙོན་དོང་ནས་འབྲོས་པ་ལྟ་བུ་ཅིག་དགོས། [27] །བར་དུ་ཤི་ཡང་མི་འགྱོད་པའི་བརྩོན་འགྲུས་ཞིང་པས་སོ་ནམ་རེམ་པ་ལྟ་བུ་ཅིག་དགོས། །ཐ་མར་ཤི་རྒྱུ་མེད་པའི་བློ་བདེ་བ་བྱ་བ་ཆླབས་ཙན་ཟིན་པའི་སྐྱེས་བུ་ལྟ་བུ་ཅིག་དགོས། །དང་པོ་ཡོང་མེད་དུ་ཤེས་པ་སྐྱེས་བུའི་གནད་ལ་མདའ་ཕོག་པ་ལྟ་བུ་ཅིག་དགོས། །བར་དུ་ཡེངས་མེད་དུ་སྒོམ་པ་བུ་གཅིག་པོ་ཤི་བའི་མ་ལྟ་བུ་ཅིག་དགོས། །ཐ་མར་བྱར་མེད་དུ་ཤེས་པ་ཤུག་མ་དགྲས་དེད་པའི་ཤི་མ་ལྟ་བུ་ཅིག་དགོས། །དང་པོ་ཆོས་ལ་ངེས་ཤེས་སྐྱེས་པ་ལྟོགས་པ་ཁ་ཟས་བཟང་པོ་དང་འཕྲད་པ་ལྟ་བུ་ཅིག་དགོས། །བར་དུ་རང་སེམས་ལ་ངེས་ཤེས་སྐྱེས་པ་གྱད་ཀྱི་ནོར་བུ་རྙེད་པ་ལྟ་བུ་ཅིག་དགོས། །ཐ་མ་གཉིས་མེད་ལ་ངེས་ཤེས་སྐྱེས་པ་ཟོག་པོ་རྫུན་ཤུག་རྟེབ་པ་ལྟ་བུ་ཅིག་དགོས། །དེ་ཁོ་ན་ཉིད་ལ་ཁོ་ཐག་ཆོད་པ་གཟེངས་ནས་འཕུར་བའི་བྱ་རོག་ལྟ་བུ་ཅིག་དགོས། །དེ་ནི་དགོས་པའི་ཆོས་བཅུ་ཡིན་ནོ། །མི་དགོས་པའི་ཆོས་བཅུ་ནི། །སེམས་ཉིད་སྟོང་པར་རྟོགས་ན་ཐོས་བསམ་བྱ་མི་དགོས། །རིག་པ་ [28] དྲི་མེད་དུ་ཤེས་ན་སྡིག་པ་སྦྱང་མི་དགོས། །རྣལ་མའི་ལམ་ལ་གནས་ན་ཚོགས་བསགས་

མི་དགོས། །གཉུག་མའི་ངང་ལ་སྐྱོང་ན་ཐབས་ལམ་བསྒོམ་མི་དགོས། །རྣམ་རྟོག་ཆོས་ཉིད་དུ་ཤེས་ན་མི་རྟོགས་པ་བསྒོམ་མི་དགོས། །ཉོན་མོངས་རྩ་བྲལ་དུ་ཤེས་ན་གཉེན་པོ་བསྟེན་མི་དགོས། །སྣང་གྲགས་སྒྱུ་མར་ཤེས་ན་དགག་སྒྲུབ་བྱ་མི་དགོས། །སྡུག་བསྔལ་དངོས་གྲུབ་ཏུ་ཤེས་ན་བདེ་བ་བཙལ་མི་དགོས། །རང་སེམས་སྐྱེ་མེད་དུ་རྟོགས་ན་འཕོ་བ་བྱ་མི་དགོས། །གང་ཡང་གཞན་དོན་དུ་བྱས་ན་རང་དོན་སྒྲུབ་མི་དགོས། །དེ་ནི་མི་དགོས་པའི་ཆོས་བཅུ་ཡིན་ནོ། །ཁྱད་པར་འཕགས་པའི་ཆོས་བཅུ་ནི། །རིགས་དྲུག་གི་སེམས་ཅན་ཇི་སྙེད་པའི་ནང་ནས་དལ་འབྱོར་དང་ལྡན་པའི་མི་ལུས་གཅིག་ཁྱད་པར་དུ་འཕགས། །མི་ནག་ཆོས་མེད་ཇི་སྙེད་པའི་ནང་ནས་ཆོས་ལྡན་གྱི་གང་ཟག་གཅིག་ཁྱད་པར་དུ་འཕགས། །ལམ་གྱི་ཐེག་པ་ཇི་སྙེད་པའི་ནང་ནས་སྙིང་པོའི་དོན་གྱི་ཐེག་པ་འདི་ཁྱད་པར་དུ་འཕགས། །ཐོས་བསམ་ལས་ [29] །བྱུང་བའི་ཤེས་རབ་ཇི་སྙེད་པ་བས་བསྒོམས་བྱུང་གི་ཤེས་རབ་སྐད་ཅིག་མ་གཅིག་ཁྱད་པར་དུ་འཕགས། །འདུས་བྱས་ཀྱི་དགེ་བ་ཇི་སྙེད་ཅིག་སྤྱད་པ་བས་འདུས་མ་བྱས་ཀྱི་དགེ་བ་སྐད་ཅིག་མ་གཅིག་ཁྱད་པར་དུ་འཕགས། །དམིགས་བཅས་ཀྱི་ཏིང་ངེ་འཛིན་ཇི་སྙེད་ཅིག་བསྒོམས་པ་བས་དམིགས་མེད་ཀྱི་ཏིང་ངེ་འཛིན་སྐད་ཅིག་ཁྱད་པར་དུ་འཕགས། །ཟག་བཅས་ཀྱི་དགེ་བ་ཇི་སྙེད་ཅིག་སྤྱད་པ་བས་ཟག་མེད་ཀྱི་དགེ་བ་སྐད་ཅིག་ཁྱད་པར་དུ་འཕགས། །རྒྱུད་ལ་ཉམས་མྱོང་ཇི་སྙེད་ཅིག་སྐྱེས་པ་བས་རྟོགས་པ་སྐད་ཅིག་ཤར་བ་ཁྱད་པར་དུ་འཕགས། །ཚེད་དུ་བྱས་པའི་ལེགས་སྤྱད་ཇི་སྙེད་ཅིག་སྤྱད་པ་བས་ཚེད་དུ་བྱ་བ་མེད་པའི་སྤྱོད་པ་སྐད་ཅིག་ཁྱད་པར་དུ་འཕགས། །ཟང་ཟིང་གི་གཏོང་འགྱེད་

ཇི་སྲིད་ཅིག་བྱས་པ་བས་དངོས་པོ་ཅི་ཡང་མ་བཟུང་བ་ཁྱད་པར་དུ་འཕགས། །དེ་ནི་ཁྱད་པར་དུ་འཕགས་པའི་ཆོས་བཅུ་ཡིན་ནོ། །ཇི་ལྟར་བྱས་ཀྱང་ལེགས་པའི་ཆོས་བཅུ་ནི། །བློ་སེམས་ [30] ཆོས་སུ་སོང་བའི་གང་ཟག་གིས། །བྱ་བ་བཏང་ཡང་ལེགས་ལ་མ་བཏང་ཡང་ལེགས། །སྒྲོ་འདོགས་སེམས་ལ་ཆོད་པའི་གང་ཟག་གིས། །བསྒོམས་ཀྱང་ལེགས་ལ་མ་བསྒོམས་ཀྱང་ལེགས། །འདོད་ཡོན་ལ་འཁྲི་བ་ཆོད་པའི་གང་ཟག་གིས། །ཆགས་མེད་བྱས་ཀྱང་ལེགས་ལ་མ་བྱས་ཀྱང་ལེགས། །ཆོས་ཉིད་མངོན་སུམ་རྟོགས་པའི་གང་ཟག་གིས། །ཕུག་སྟོང་དུ་ཉལ་ཡང་ལེགས་ལ་མང་པོའི་ཚོགས་དཔོན་བྱས་ཀྱང་ལེགས། །སྣང་བ་སྒྱུ་མར་ཤེས་པའི་གང་ཟག་གིས། །གཅིག་པུར་རི་ཁྲོད་དུ་བསྡད་ཀྱང་ལེགས་ལ་རྒྱལ་ཁམས་ཕྱོགས་མེད་བསྐོར་ཡང་ལེགས། །སེམས་ལ་རང་དབང་ཐོབ་པའི་གང་ཟག་གིས། །འདོད་པའི་ཡོན་ཏན་སྤངས་ཀྱང་ལེགས་ལ་བསྟེན་ཀྱང་ལེགས། །བྱང་ཆུབ་ཀྱི་སེམས་དང་ལྡན་པའི་གང་ཟག་གིས། །དབེན་པར་སྒྲུབ་པ་བྱས་ཀྱང་ལེགས་ལ་ཚོགས་སུ་གཞན་དོན་བྱས་ཀྱང་ལེགས། །མོས་གུས་ཐང་ལྷོད་མེད་པའི་གང་ཟག་གིས། །བླ་མའི་ཞབས་དྲུང་དུ་བསྡད་ཀྱང་ལེགས་ལ་མ་བསྡད་ཀྱང་ལེགས། །མང་དུ་ཐོས་ཤིང་དོན་གོ་བར་ [31] །ལྡན་པའི་གང་ཟག་ལ། །དངོས་གྲུབ་བྱུང་ཡང་ལེགས་ལ་བར་ཆད་བྱུང་ཡང་ལེགས། །རྟོགས་པ་མཆོག་ཐོབ་པའི་རྣལ་འབྱོར་པ་ལ། །ཐུན་མོང་གི་གྲུབ་རྟགས་ཡོད་ཀྱང་ལེགས་ལ་མེད་ཀྱང་ལེགས། །དེ་ནི་ཇི་ལྟར་བྱས་ཀྱང་ལེགས་པའི་ཆོས་བཅུ་ཡིན་ནོ། །དམ་པའི་ཆོས་ཀྱི་ཡོན་ཏན་བཅུ་ནི། །ཆོས་དགེ་བ་བཅུ་དང་། ཕ་རོལ་ཏུ་ཕྱིན་པ་དྲུག་པོ་དང་། །སྟོང་པ་

ཉིད་ཐམས་ཅད་དང་། །བྱང་ཆུབ་ཀྱི་ཕྱོགས་ཀྱི་ཆོས་རྣམས་དང་། །འཕགས་པའི་
བདེན་པ་བཞི་དང་། །བསམ་གཏན་བཞི་དང་། །གཟུགས་མེད་པའི་སྙོམས་པར་
འཇུག་པ་བཞི་དང་། །སྔགས་ཀྱི་སྨིན་གྲོལ་ལ་སོགས་པ་རྣམས་འཇིག་རྟེན་དུ་འབྱུང་
བ་ནི་དམ་པའི་ཆོས་ཀྱི་ཡོན་ཏན་ནོ། །མིའི་ནང་ནས་རྒྱལ་རིགས་ཆེ་ཞིང་མཐོ་
བ་དང་། །བྲམ་ཟེའི་རིགས་ཆེ་ཞིང་མཐོ་བ་དང་། །ཁྱིམ་བདག་གི་རིགས་ཆེ་ཞིང་
མཐོ་བ་དང་། །རྒྱལ་ཆེན་བཞི་ལ་སོགས་པ་འདོད་ཁམས་ཀྱི་ལྷ་རིགས་དྲུག་དང་།
།གཟུགས་ཁམས་ཀྱི་ལྷ་རིགས་བཅུ་བདུན་དང་གཟུགས་མེད་པའི་ལྷ་རིགས་བཞི་
འཇིག་རྟེན་ན་འབྱུང་ [32] བ་ནི་དམ་པའི་ཆོས་ཀྱི་ཡོན་ཏན་ཡིན་ནོ། །རྒྱུན་
དུ་ཞུགས་པ་དང་། །ལན་གཅིག་ཕྱིར་འོང་བ་དང་། ཕྱིར་མི་འོང་བ་དང་། དགྲ་
བཅོམ་པ་དང་རང་སངས་རྒྱས་དང་། །རྣམ་པ་ཐམས་ཅད་མཁྱེན་པའི་སངས་
རྒྱས་འཇིག་རྟེན་དུ་བྱོན་ཞིང་འབྱུང་བ་ནི་དམ་པའི་ཆོས་ཀྱི་ཡོན་ཏན་ཡིན་ནོ།
།སེམས་བསྐྱེད་དང་སྨོན་ལམ་གྱི་སྟོབས་ཀྱིས་ཐུགས་རྗེ་རང་ཤར་གྱི་གཟུགས་སྐུ་
གཉིས་ཀྱིས་ཇི་སྲིད་འཁོར་བ་མ་སྟོངས་ཀྱི་བར་དུ་སེམས་ཅན་གྱི་དོན་ལྷུན་གྲུབ་
དུ་འབྱུང་བ་ནི་དམ་པའི་ཆོས་ཀྱི་ཡོན་ཏན་ཡིན་ནོ། །སེམས་ཅན་ཉེ་བར་འཚོ་
བའི་ཡོ་བྱད་གང་ལ་གང་འོས་པ་ཕུན་སུམ་ཚོགས་པ་ཐམས་ཅད་ནི་བྱང་ཆུབ་
སེམས་དཔའ་རྣམས་ཀྱི་སྨོན་ལམ་གྱི་སྟོབས་ལས་བྱུང་བས་ན་དམ་པའི་ཆོས་
ཀྱི་ཡོན་ཏན་ཡིན་ནོ། །ངན་སོང་དང་མི་ཁོམ་པའི་གནས་ན་ཡང་གནས་སྐབས་
ཀྱི་བདེ་བ་ཅུང་ཟད་ཡོད་པ་དེ་དག་ཐམས་ཅད་ཀྱང་དཀར་པོ་དགེ་བའི་བསོད་
ནམས་ལས་གྲུབ་པས་ན་དམ་པའི་ཆོས་ཀྱི་ཡོན་ཏན་ཡིན་ནོ། །སྐྱེས་བུ་ངན་པ་

དག་ཀྱང་དམ་པའི་ཆོས་སུ་བློ་ [33] །འགྱུར་ནས་སྐྱེས་བུ་དམ་པའི་རིགས་སུ་གནས་ཤིང་། །མི་ཀུན་གྱི་གཙུག་ཏུ་འཁུར་བའི་གནས་སུ་གྱུར་པ་ནི་དམ་པའི་ཆོས་ཀྱི་ཡོན་ཏན་ཡིན་ནོ། །སྔར་སྡིག་པ་མི་དགེ་བ་ལ་བག་མེད་དུ་སྤྱོད་ཅིང་དམྱལ་བའི་བུད་ཤིང་གི་རྒྱུ་སོགས་པ་དེ་ཡང་། །དམ་པའི་ཆོས་ཀྱི་ཕྱོགས་སུ་བློ་ལྟ་འགྱུར་ནས་མཐོ་རིས་དང་ཐར་པའི་བདེ་བ་ལ་རེག་པར་གྱུར་པ་ནི་དམ་པའི་ཆོས་ཀྱི་ཡོན་ཏན་ཡིན་ནོ། །དམ་པའི་ཆོས་ལ་དད་པ་ཙམ་མམ། མོས་པ་ཙམ་མམ། །དགའ་བ་ཙམ་མམ། །ཆ་ལུགས་འཛིན་པ་ཙམ་ཡང་ཀུན་གྱིས་ཡིད་དུ་འོང་ཞིང་། །བསྙེན་བཀུར་གྱི་གནས་སུ་གྱུར་པ་ནི་དམ་པའི་ཆོས་ཀྱི་ཡོན་ཏན་ཡིན་ནོ། །བདོག་པའི་དངོས་པོ་ཐམས་ཅད་སྤངས་ནས་ཁྱིམ་ནས་ཁྱིམ་མེད་པར་རབ་ཏུ་བྱུང་ཞིང་། །རི་ཁྲོད་དགོན་པ་དག་ཏུ་ཡིབས་ནས་བསྡད་ཀྱང་འཚོ་བའི་ཡོ་བྱད་ཕུན་སུམ་ཚོགས་པར་འབྱུང་བ་ནི་དམ་པའི་ཆོས་ཀྱི་ཡོན་ཏན་ཡིན་ནོ། །དེ་ནི་དམ་པའི་ཆོས་ཀྱི་ཡོན་ཏན་མདོར་བསྡུས་པའི་ཆོས་བཅུ་ཡིན་ནོ། །མིང་ [34] ཙམ་གྱི་ཆོས་བཅུ་ནི། །གཞིའི་གནས་ལུགས་བསྟན་དུ་མེད་པས་གཞི་མིང་ཙམ་ཡིན། །ལམ་ལ་བགྲོད་བྱ་བགྲོད་བྱེད་མེད་པས་ལམ་མིང་ཙམ་ཡིན། །གནས་ལུགས་ལ་བལྟ་བྱ་ལྟ་བྱེད་མེད་པས་རྟོགས་པ་མིང་ཙམ་ཡིན། །གཉུག་མ་ལ་བསྒོམ་བྱ་སྒོམ་བྱེད་མེད་པས་ཉམས་མྱོང་མིང་ཙམ་ཡིན། །གཤིས་ལ་སྤྱད་བྱ་སྤྱོད་བྱེད་མེད་པས་སྤྱོད་པ་མིང་ཙམ་ཡིན། །དོན་ལ་བསྲུང་བྱ་སྲུང་བྱེད་མེད་པས་དམ་ཚིག་མིང་ཙམ་ཡིན། །དོན་ལ་བསག་བྱ་གསོག་བྱེད་མེད་པས་ཚོགས་གཉིས་མིང་ཙམ་ཡིན། །དོན་ལ་སྦྱང་བྱ་སྦྱོང་བྱེད་མེད་པས་སྒྲིབ་གཉིས་མིང་ཙམ་ཡིན། །དོན་ལ་སྤང་བྱ་

སྐྱོང་བྱེད་མེད་པས་འཁོར་བ་མིང་ཙམ་ཡིན། །དོན་ལ་ཐོབ་བྱ་ཐོབ་བྱེད་མེད་པས་འབྲས་བུ་མིང་ཙམ་ཡིན། །དེ་ནི་མིང་ཙམ་གྱི་ཆོས་བཅུ་ཡིན་ནོ། །བདེ་བ་ཆེན་པོར་ལྷུན་གྱིས་གྲུབ་པའི་ཆོས་བཅུ་ནི། །སེམས་ཅན་ཐམས་ཅད་ཀྱི་སེམས་ཀྱི་རང་བཞིན་ཆོས་སྐུར་གནས་པས་བདེ་བ་ཆེན་པོར་ལྷུན་གྱིས་གྲུབ། །གཞི་ཆོས་ཉིད་ཀྱི་དབྱིངས་ [35] །ལས་མཚན་མའི་སྒྲིབ་པ་མེད་པས་བདེ་བ་ཆེན་པོར་ལྷུན་གྱིས་གྲུབ། །མཐའ་བྲལ་བློ་འདས་ཀྱི་རྟོགས་པ་ལ་ཕྱོགས་རིས་ཀྱི་སྒྲིབ་པ་མེད་པས་བདེ་བ་ཆེན་པོར་ལྷུན་གྱིས་གྲུབ། །ཡིད་ལ་བྱ་བ་མེད་པའི་ཉམས་སྐྱོང་ལ་དམིགས་པའི་སྒྲིབ་པ་མེད་པས་བདེ་བ་ཆེན་པོར་ལྷུན་གྱིས་གྲུབ། །བྱ་བྲལ་རྩོལ་མེད་ཀྱི་སྤྱོད་པ་ལ་བླང་དོར་གྱི་སྒྲིབ་པ་མེད་པས་བདེ་བ་ཆེན་པོར་ལྷུན་གྱིས་གྲུབ། །དབྱིངས་དང་ཡེ་ཤེས་དབྱེར་མེད་པའི་ཆོས་སྐུ་ལ་གཟུང་འཛིན་གྱི་སྒྲིབ་པ་མེད་པས་བདེ་བ་ཆེན་པོར་ལྷུན་གྱིས་གྲུབ། །ཐུགས་རྗེ་རང་བྱུང་གི་ལོངས་སྐུ་ལ་སྐྱེ་ཤི་འཕོ་འགྱུར་གྱི་སྒྲིབ་པ་མེད་པས་བདེ་བ་ཆེན་པོར་ལྷུན་གྱིས་གྲུབ། །ཐུགས་རྗེ་རང་ཤར་གྱི་སྤྲུལ་སྐུ་ལ་གཉིས་སྣང་འདུ་བྱེད་ཀྱི་སྒྲིབ་པ་མེད་པས་བདེ་བ་ཆེན་པོར་ལྷུན་གྱིས་གྲུབ། །བསྟན་པ་ཆོས་ཀྱི་འཁོར་ལོ་ལ་བདག་ལྟ་མཚན་མའི་སྒྲིབ་པ་མེད་པས་བདེ་བ་ཆེན་པོར་ལྷུན་གྱིས་གྲུབ། །ཚད་མེད་ཐུགས་རྗེའི་ཕྲིན་ལས་ལ་རྒྱ་ཆད་དུས་ཚིགས་མེད་པས་ [36] བདེ་བ་ཆེན་པོར་ལྷུན་གྱིས་གྲུབ་པ་སྟེ། །དེ་ནི་བདེ་བ་ཆེན་པོར་ལྷུན་གྱིས་གྲུབ་པའི་ཆོས་བཅུ་ཡིན་ནོ། །ཟག་མེད་མཁྱེན་པ་དང་ལྡན་པའི་བླ་མ་དང་། །རྗེ་བཙུན་སྒྲོལ་མ་ལ་སོགས་ལྷག་པའི་ལྷ་རྣམས་ཀྱིས་བྱང་ཕྱོགས་ཁ་བ་ཅན་གྱི་བསྟན་པའི་གསལ་བྱེད་དུ་མངའ་གསོལ་

བའི་དཔལ་ལྡན་མར་མི་མཛད་ཡབ་སྲས་ཀྱི་གསུང་རྒྱུན་དྲི་མ་མེད་པ་རྣམས་
བཀའ་གདམས་པའི་སླ་མ་སྐུ་དྲིན་ཅན་རྣམས་ལས་ཐོས་པ་དང་། །རྒྱ་གར་འཕགས་
པའི་ཡུལ་དུ་ཉི་ཟླ་ལྟར་གྲགས་པའི་སྐྱེས་མཆོག་ནཱ་རོ་མཻ་ཏྲི་གཉིས་དང་། མར་
པ་ལྷོ་བྲག་པ་ལ་སོགས་པའི་མཁས་གྲུབ་རྣམས་ཀྱི་ཐུགས་ཀྱི་བཅུད་འཛིན་པ་རྗེ་
བཙུན་གྱི་རྒྱལ་པོ་མི་ལ་རས་པས་རྗེས་སུ་བཟུང་བའི་གསུང་དྲི་མ་མེད་པ་རྣམས་
ཕྱོགས་གཅིག་ཏུ་བསྡུས་པའི་ལམ་མཆོག་རིན་པོ་ཆེའི་ཕྲེང་བ་ཅེས་བྱ་བ། །བཀའ་
ཕྱག་གཉིས་ཀྱིས་གདམས་པའི་མཛོད་འཆང་བ་ཤར་དྭགས་པོ་སྙི་སྒོམ་བསོད་
ནམས་རིན་ཆེན་གྱིས་བྲིས་པ་རྫོགས་སོ།། །།རྗེ་སྒམ་ [37] པོ་པའི་ཞལ་
ནས། མ་འོངས་པའི་གང་ཟག་བདག་ལ་མོས་ཤིང་བདག་དང་མ་འཕྲད་སྙམ་
པ་ཀུན་ཀྱང་། ཁོ་བོས་བརྩམས་པའི་ལམ་མཆོག་རིན་པོ་ཆེའི་ཕྲེང་བ་དང་། ཐར་
པ་རིན་པོ་ཆེའི་རྒྱན་ལ་སོགས་བསྟན་བཅོས་རྣམས་གཟིགས་པར་ཞུ། ང་དང་
མངོན་སུམ་དུ་འཕྲད་པ་དང་ཁྱད་པར་མེད་པར་ཡོད་ཀྱི་གསུངས་འདུག་པས། །རྗེ་
སྒམ་པོ་པ་ལ་མོས་པའི་སྐལ་ལྡན་རྣམས་ཀྱིས་འདི་དག་སྐྱེལ་བའི་ལས་ལ་བརྩོན་
པར་ཞུའོ། །རྒྱལ་བ་གང་དེའི་བསྟན་པའི་ཉི་མ་ཆེ། །འཛམ་གླིང་གྲགས་དེ་འགྲོ་
ལ་རྗེས་ཆགས་པས། །ལམ་གྱི་མཆོག་གྱུར་རིན་ཆེན་ཕྲེང་བ་འདི། །ཚེ་འདིར་
བསྟན་ལ་བྱ་བ་བྱེད་ཕྱིར་དང་། །རིང་ནས་མཁའ་མཉམ་དྲིན་ཆེན་ཕ་མ་རྣམས།
།དོན་གཉིས་འགྲུབ་ནས་མངོན་པར་སངས་རྒྱས་ཏེ། །རྒྱལ་བསྟན་བཤད་སྒྲུབ་
ཕྱོགས་མཐར་བརྡལ་བའི་ཕྱིར། །སྤར་དུ་གསར་བསྐྲུན་ཀརྨའི་ཆོས་སྒར་དུ།
།བཞུགས་འདི་གསལ་ལ་དད་ལྡན་སྒྲོན་མེར་ཤོག། །སརྦ་མངྒ་ལཾ།།

Notes

1. See Jampa Mackenzie Stewart, *The Life of Gampopa*, Ithaca: Snow Lion, 1995.

2. See Jamgon Kongtrul, *The Great Path of Awakening*, Boston: Shambhala, 1987.

3. See The Ninth Karmapa, *Mahamudra, Eliminating the Darkness of Ignorance*, Dharamsala: Library of Tibetan Works and Archives, 1978; and Jamgon Kongtrul, *Cloudless Sky*, Boston: Shambhala, 1992.

4. sGam-po-pa, *The Jewel Ornament of Liberation*, tr. by Herbert V. Guenther, Boulder: Prajña, 1971; and Gampopa, *Gems of Dharma, Jewels of Freedom*, tr. by Ken and Katia Holmes, Forres, Scotland: Altea, 1995.

5. W. Y. Evans-Wentz, ed., *Tibetan Yoga and Secret Doctrines*, London: Oxford, 1958, p. 67; and Gampopa, *The Precious Garland of the Sublime Path*, Boudenath: Rangjung Yeshe, 1995.

6. The age of decadence is a period characterized by a degeneration in views and conduct.

7. The *eight freedoms* are not being born as: a hell being, hungry ghost, animal, barbarian, long-lived god, heretic, being in a dark age, or a mute. Of the *ten resources*, the *five personal resources* are: having a human body, being born in a land where the Dharma has spread, having intact sense organs, having encountered the Dharma, having confidence in the Three Jewels. The *five resources from others* are that: the Buddha has been born in this age, he has taught, the Dharma has not declined, there are many followers, and there are benevolent sponsors.

8. *Bodhicitta,* "the mind of enlightenment," combines unlimited loving-kindness and compassion toward all sentient beings with the wisdom of seeing that all things are empty of self-existence.

9. Vajradhara is the "Dharmakaya Buddha," considered the origin of the Kagyu lineage.

10. *Ngöndro* are the preliminary or foundation practices for the vajrayana. The *four ordinary foundations* or the *four thoughts that turn the mind toward the Dharma* are contemplation of the precious human birth, impermanence, the cause and effect of karma, and the sufferings of samsara. The *four extraordinary foundations* are: prostrations for taking refuge and generating bodhicitta; Vajrasattva mantra recitation for purification; mandala offerings for generating merit; and guru yoga for receiving the blessings of the lineage.

11. The eight worldly dharmas are gain and loss, pleasure and pain, praise and blame, and fame and infamy.

12. Dewachen, or Sukhavati in Sanskrit, is the pure land where Amitabha Buddha resides.

13. Maras are obstacles to Dharma practice. These "maras" or obstacles are traditionally personified as "Mara," the tempter, demon, or devil. The four maras are: *skandha-mara,* the belief that the five aggregates (form, feeling, perception, concepts, and consciousness) constitute a self; *klesha-mara,* the negative emotions; *mrityu-mara,* death; and *devaputra-mara,* seduction by the bliss of meditation.

14. The *three realms* are the desire, form, and formless realms. The desire realm includes six levels of gods, in addition to the hell, hungry ghost, animal, human, and demigod realms. The form realm includes seventeen higher levels of gods, and the formless realm includes the four highest levels of gods.

15. The *six states of existence* are the hell being, hungry ghost, animal, human, demigod, and god realms.

16. The *three types of suffering* are the suffering of suffering, the suffering of change, and the suffering of conditioned existence.

17. *The Profound Inner Meaning* (*Zab mo nang dön*) is a work by the Third Karmapa, Rangjung Dorje. Khenpo Karthar gave an oral commentary on this work in the summers of 1989 and 1990 at Karma Triyana Dharmachakra.

18. *Mani* stones are stones carved with the mantra, "Om mani peme hung," the mantra of Chenrezig, the bodhisattva of compassion.

19. The four root violations of moral conduct, or *the four roots*, are killing, stealing, lying, and sexual misconduct.

20. In mahayana, it is emphasized that compassionate action, described as method or skillful means, leads to the accumulation of merit. In vajrayana, the practices themselves also generate vast merit, and are described as method. In either case, it is important to combine method with wisdom.

21. The heading of this section in the Tibetan wood block edition states that there are twelve points, but there appear to be only eleven distinct points actually listed.

22. *The Rain of Wisdom*, tr. by Nalanda Translation Committee, Boston: Shambhala, 1989.

23. The *ten virtuous actions* are the opposites of the ten unvirtuous actions: ill-will, coveting, wrong views, harsh words, slander, idle speech, killing, stealing, sexual misconduct.

24. The *four dhyanas* are four levels of tranquility meditation. They are related to the realm of form, and attachment to their practice may lead to rebirth in the realm of form.

25. The *four formless absorptions* are further levels of tranquility meditation, which are related to the formless realm, the highest of the three realms of samsara.

26. *Subsequent attainment* means post-meditation.

27. *Superimposition* means adding something to appearances that is not really present, such as a permanent, unitary self, or the inherent existence of things.

28. The *four unities* are appearance and emptiness, sound and emptiness, bliss and emptiness, and awareness and emptiness.